ROSALYN YALOW

Scientist With A Fighting Spirit

DR. CHANCHAL KUMAR MANNA

INDIA • SINGAPORE • MALAYSIA

Copyright © Dr. Chanchal Kumar Manna 2023
All Rights Reserved.

ISBN 979-8-89133-372-7

Dedication

"The excitement of learning separates youth from old age. As long as you're learning, you're not old."

Wise words from Rosalyn Yalow, a Nobel Prize-awarded nuclear physicist who revolutionised the medical world by developing radioimmunoassay technique. In 2011, she passed away aged 89.

The Author of this Book pays his respect to Professor Rosalyn Yalow, — who had a fighting spirit throughout life.

Contents

Acknowledgements

"A Book is a gift you can open again and again"

– Garrison Keillor

"The sustaining interest and enthusiasm of many friends and colleagues are, of course, the nutrition that every writer needs, and can never adequately acknowledge."

– Philip Ball

Writing a book is harder than I thought and more rewarding than I could have ever imagined. None of this would have been possible without the help of some of my friends. They stood by me during every struggle and all my successes. That is true friendship.

First and foremost, I would like to praise and thank God, the Almighty, who has granted countless blessing, knowledge, and opportunity to the writer, so that I have been finally able to accomplish the Book. Apart from the efforts of me, the success of this Book depends largely on the encouragement and guidelines of many others. I take this opportunity to express my gratitude to the people who have been instrumental in the successful completion of this Book. It would be impossible to list all names but several people deserve his sincere and special thanks.

Nobody has been more important to me in the pursuit of this project than the members of my family. This journey would not have been possible without the support of my family, mentors, and friends. Most importantly, I wish to thank my loving and supportive wife, Samita, and my two wonderful daughters, Sukanya and Sulagna and loving Grandson, Rishan, who provided unending inspiration.

– Dr. Chanchal Kumar Manna

Preface

The author of this book is very humble in writing some aspects about one stubborn, determined, and talented Jewish woman. Her name is Rosalyn Sussman Yalow (born July 19, 1921,New York, U. S.). From the very beginning of her life, she fought with poverty in every sphere of her life. She was an American medical physicist and winner of the 1977 Nobel Prize in Physiology or Medicine for the development of a technique known as radioimmunoassay (RIA). Whenever we like to discuss about RIA, the name of another renowned person comes in. Hisname is Solomon Berson. Solomon Berson, a talented resident who joined the radioisotope unit and within four years became its chief. Yalow and Berson began a research partnership that was to last 22 years, until Berson's untimely death in 1972. In 1977 their discovery was awarded the Nobel Prize for Medicine. The technique "brought a revolution in biological and medical research," the Karolinska Institute in Sweden said in awarding Dr. Yalow, along with Andrew V. Schally, M. D., Ph. D., and Roger Guillemin, M. D., Ph. D., the Nobel Prize in 1977. (Dr. Berson would have shared the prize but he died before the award was given.)

Rosalyn S. Yalow became the second woman to ever win the Nobel Prize in medicine, 1977. Her achievement was the development of RIA, an application of nuclear physics in clinical medicine. She invented this technique in 1959 to measure the amount of insulin in the blood of adult diabetics.

She was born on July 19, 1921, in New York City, of Jewish parents, Clara and Simon Sussman. She attended the New York City public school system and in Walton High School. She graduated from Hunter

College and accepted a teaching fellowship in physics at the University of Illinois. In 1945, she became the second woman to receive a Ph. D. degree in physics from Illinois.

After World War II, the Veterans Administration was interested in doing research to explore the possible use of radioactive substances in the diagnosis of treatment and diseases. The VA Hospital in the Bronx was chosen as one of the sites where research would be conducted. Dr. Yalow, who was a consultant in this facility, was hired to work on nuclear physics in 1947. In 1950, she was appointed physicist and assistant chief of the hospital's radioisotope service.

With a colleague, the American physician Solomon A. Berson, Yalow began using radioactive isotopes to examine and diagnose various disease conditions. Yalow and Berson's investigations into the mechanism underlying type II diabetes led to their development of RIA.

Afterward, she moved to the Bronx Veterans Administration (VA) Hospital, where she helped set up its cutting-edge radioisotope lab. Working alongside colleague Solomon Berson,she developed radioimmunoassay (RIA), a technique that can measure one-trillionth of a gram of material per millilitre of blood. Because of the small sample required for measurement, RIA quickly became a standard laboratory tool all over the world today.

Before this revolutionary break through, scientists could only analyse reactions between antigens and antibodies and those that produced visible precipitation or other evidence, such as the clumping of red blood cells. The RIA method revolutionized endocrinology—the study of ductless glands and hormones – and the treatment of disorders like diabetes. For the first time, doctors could diagnose conditions caused by minute changes in hormones and treat conditions with hormones.

In 1977, Yalow was the sixth individual woman (seventh overall, considering MarieCurie's two wins), and first American-born woman, to win the Nobel Prize in a scientific field. She was also the second woman in the world to win in the physiology or medicine category, the first being Gerty Cori in 1947 for her role in the discovery of glycogen metabolism.

She received the Nobel Prize five years after Berson's death. Berson probably would have been honoured alongside her, but Nobel Prizes are not given posthumously. Following his death. Rosalyn's great regret was that she was not able to share it with her colleague, who died suddenly of a heart attack on 11 April, 1972. Yalow requested that the laboratory where they both worked should be renamed in his honour. Shortly afterwards, the laboratory in which the two scientists had worked for many years was named, at her request, in memory of Doctor Berson.

The commercial possibilities for RIA were enormous, but while Yalow and Berson recognized this, they refused to patent the method. Instead, they made every effort to get RIA into common use, putting its value to humanity ahead of their own financial interests. Yalow asserted, "We never thought of patenting RIA.... patents are about keeping things away from people for the purpose of making money. We wanted others to be able to use RIA." The seemingly inextricable connection between money and medicine was never a primary concern to Yalow.

As a woman, Rosalyn had to overcome many obstacles before being able to devote her life full-time to scientific research. Married to her colleague Aaron Yalow and a mother to two children, even after achieving success in her career, Rosalyn never stopped fighting against female discrimination. She strived for women to always be guaranteed equal opportunities in accessing education and was known to encourage young female students to pursue scientific careers.

During her extraordinary scientific career, Rosalyn became a mentor and reference point for scientists from around the world, who came to share her passion for investigative endocrinology research. This is why she has been called **the mother of endocrinology**.

During her hectic life as a scientist and as the wife and mother of a family, she managed to host a five-part dramatic series on the life of Madame Curie, for the Public Broadcasting Service in 1976. She has put in long hours each week at the VA. Hospital and then come home to her kosher kitchen to prepare meals for her family. Dr. Yalow displayed energy and enthusiasm at all times for work and family. Dr. Rosalyn Yalow was a beacon and guide for young women in achieving position and recognition in life. She demonstrated through her life that it is possible for a woman to be an outstanding professional as well as have a good family in their lifetime.

What led Dr. Yalow to such amazing success? Well, hershort autobiography, published on the Nobel Prize Website, offers a glimpse. "Through the years my mother hastoldme that it was fortunate that I chose to do acceptable things, for if I had chosen otherwise no one could have deflected me from my path," wrote Dr. Yalow herself on the website **www.nobelprize.org**. She also called herself a "stubborn, determined child." Possibly, therein lay the secret of her triumph over adversity and her path to success.

Even after receiving the Nobel Prize, Rosalyn continued at full capacity with her research, which led to the award of other prestigious acknowledgements: in 1988 she received the National Medal of Science, the highest honour reserved for US citizens who have made important contributions to science and technology.

Rosalyn Yalow has always worked to further the role of women in science, in particular observing that among the scientists, scholars, and leaders of the world. She also emphasized the need of women scientists for day care in order to pursue advanced education and research. "It's a tragedy for society," she has said, "when talented women do not have children." She always tried to make women aware of the necessity of working towards the goal of achieving their due status: An outspoken promoter of equal opportunity, she criticized reverse discrimination, and refused the Woman of the Year award of Ladies' Home Journal because she thought men and women should compete on equal terms and not be considered remarkable because of their gender.

– Dr. Yalow died on May 30, 2011, at the age of 89.

Summary

Rosalyn Yalow, (1921–2011) aged 89, trained in physics and never took a course in biology. From the very beginning of her life, she fought with poverty in every sphere of her life. She was an American medical physicist and winner of the 1977 Nobel Prize in Physiology or Medicine, for the development of a technique known as radioimmunoassay (RIA). Whenever we like to discuss about RIA, the name of another renowned person comes in. His name is Solomon Berson. Solomon Berson, a talented resident who joined the radioisotope unit and began a research partnership with Yalow that was to last 22 years, until Berson's untimely death in 1972. In 1977 their discovery was awarded the Nobel Prize for Medicine.

She was born on July 19, 1921, in New York City, of Jewish parents, Clara and Simon Sussman. She attended the New York City public school system and in Walton High School. She graduated from Hunter College and accepted a teaching fellowship in physics at the University of Illinois. In 1945, she became the second woman to receive a Ph. D. degree in physics from Illinois. From 1946 to 1950 she lectured on physics at Hunter, and in 1947 she became a consultant in nuclear physics to the Bronx Veterans Administration Hospital, where from 1950 to 1970 she was physicist and assistant chief of the radioisotope service.

With a colleague, the American physician Solomon A. Berson, Yalow began using radioactive isotopes to examine and diagnose various disease conditions. Yalow and Berson's investigations into the mechanism underlying type II diabetes led to their development of RIA. Their collaboration led to outstanding scientific results: for the first time, Rosalyn Yalow and Solomon Berson developed RIA (Radio Immunoassay) a diagnostic technique that is still used all over the world today.

In 1977, Yalow was the sixth individual woman (seventh overall, considering Marie Curie's two wins), and first American-born woman, to win the Nobel Prize in a scientific field. She received the Nobel Prize five years after Berson's death. She was also the second woman in the world to win in the physiology or medicine category, the first being Gerty Cori in 1947 for her role in the discovery of glycogen metabolism.

As a woman, Rosalyn had to overcome many obstacles before being able to devote her life full-time to scientific research. Married to her colleague Aaron Yalow and a mother of two children, even after achieving success in her career, Rosalyn never stopped fighting against female discrimination. She strived for women to always be guaranteed equal opportunities in accessing education and was known to encourage young female students to pursue scientific careers.

Even after receiving the Nobel Prize, Rosalyn continued at full capacity with her research, which led to the award of other prestigious acknowledgements: in 1988 she received the National Medal of Science, the highest honour reserved for US citizens who have made important contributions to science and technology.

Rosalyn Yalow has always worked to further the role of women in science. She also emphasized the need of women scientists for day care in order to pursue advanced education and research. Dr. Rosalyn Yalow was a beacon and guide for young women in achieving position and recognition in life. She demonstrated through her life that it is possible for a woman to be an outstanding professional as well as have a good family in their lifetime.

– Dr. Yalow died on May 30, 2011, at age 89.

ROSALYN YALOW

Fig 1. Rosalyn Yalow (1921–2011)
(winner of the 1977 Nobel Prize in Physiology or Medicine)

Dr. Rosalyn Yalow (1921–2011)

A woman of many achievements, Rosalyn Yalow, Ph. D., was a medical physicist who co-developed the radioimmunoassay (RIA) technique for measuring hormones and other biological substances and became the second woman to win the Nobel Prize in Physiology or Medicine. Dr. Yalow was also the first female and first Nobel Laureate to become President of The Endocrine Society (1978–1979).

Radioimmunoassay is a sensitive method for measuring very small amounts of a substance in the blood. Radioactive versions of a substance, or isotopes of a substance, are mixed with antibodies and inserted in a sample of the patient's blood. The same non-radioactive substance in the blood takes the place of the isotope in the antibodies, thus leaving the radioactive substance free. The amount of free isotope is then measured to see how much of the original substance was in the blood. Radioimmunoassay is used to measure concentrations of hormones, viruses, enzymes, and many other substances in the blood. It is widely used in medicine today. The test can also be used to measure the levels of vitamins and viruses. Today, blood banks use it to screen blood for the hepatitis virus. RIA and its variation called ELISA, which uses enzymes or fluorescent markers, are widely used in medical and clinical research labs.

This measuring method was developed by two VA researchers, Dr. Rosalyn Yalow (who received the Nobel Prize in Physiology or Medicine for her work in 1977) and Dr. Solomon Berson, who died in 1972 and was not eligible for the Nobel, which is not awarded posthumously.

The radioimmunoassay (RIA) technique — for which Rosalyn Sussman Yalow received a share of a Nobel prize in 1977 — has revolutionized almost every field of medicine. It uses radioisotope tracers to measure the concentration of tiny amounts of substances in the blood and other body fluids. Being able to measure levels of hormones, drugs, vitamins, and viruses suddenly made it possible for researchers and clinicians to diagnose problems and treat patients with appropriate doses of medication, and to probe the causes of numerous diseases.

Rationale of Developing RIA Technique

The research collaboration consisted of Dr. Yalow's expertise in nuclear counting techniques and Dr. Berson's clinical expertise on diabetes made a revolution in Medical Science. Their first project used radioisotopes to estimate blood volume. However, their first major contribution was a study of how the thyroid gland and kidneys remove iodine from the blood. They then applied their methods to insulin. Dr. Yalow had a personal interest in insulin, because her husband suffered from diabetes. Dr. Yalow and Dr. Berson were the first to prove that peptides such as insulin could stimulate an immunologic response or the production of antibodies. This finding was not readily accepted in the scientific community because it was believed that peptides were too small to be recognized by the immune system. They had difficulty publishing the paper, but succeeded in 1959. Soon others confirmed their data and their work's significance became known.

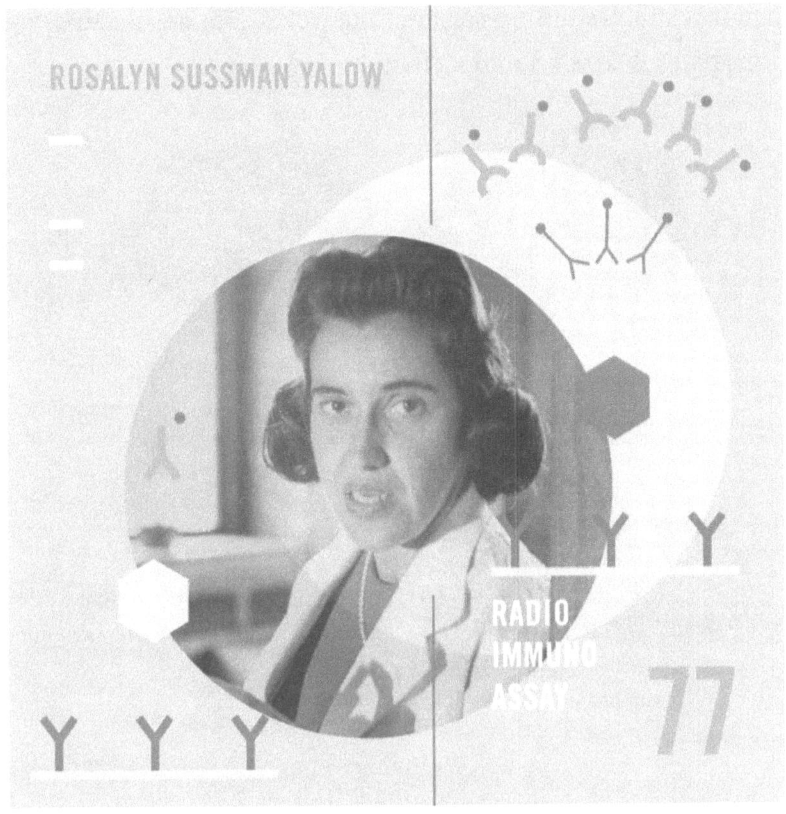

Fig. 2. Rosalyn Sussman Yalow was the winner of the 1977 Nobel Prize in Physiology or Medicine

Rosalyn Sussman Yalow was an American medical physicist and winner of the 1977 Nobel Prize in Physiology or Medicine for the development of the radioimmunoassay (RIA) technique. RIA is a technique used to measure minute quantities of hormones and other antigens in the human body. Rosalyn first used it to study insulin levels in diabetes mellitus but it has been widely used in a number of detection screens, from looking for the presence of drugs to identifying certain disease or allergy markers like peptic ulcers. The process involves "tagging" or labelling known antigens with radioactive isotopes so they can be easily identified. RIA is considered the pioneer in nuclear medicine radioactive measurements because radioactive substances show up with great accuracy and clarity.

Though it is still used in labs around the world, labs are shifting towards methods that rely less on radioactivity.

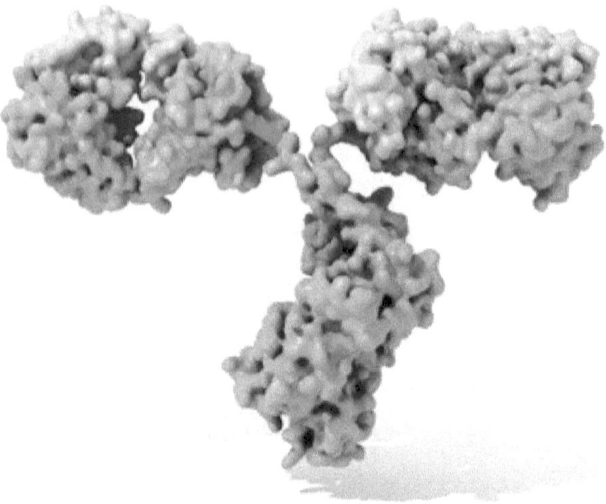

Fig.3. A 3D model of an Immunoglobulin molecule, showing heavy chains in blue and light chains in green.

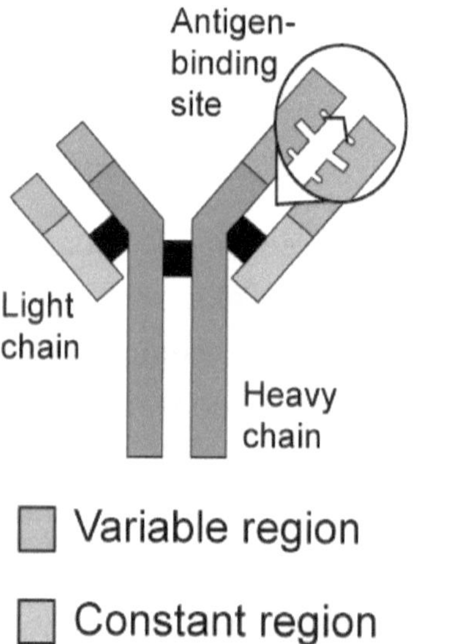

Fig.4. Antibody structure schematic. An antibody is made up of two heavy chains and two light chains. The variable region, which differs from one antibody to the next, allows an antibody to recognize its matching antigen.

Radioimmunoassay

The most famous discovery made by Berson and Yalow was a technique called radioimmunoassay, or RIA, a method of quantifying minute amounts of biological substances in the body using radioactive – labelled material. Measuring the concentrations of various chemical compounds in the human body is important for diagnosing diseases and for making sure a medicine is working properly, but many compounds are present in the blood in such low concentrations that measuring them can be difficult. RIA makes the job much easier.

With RIA a known quantity of the substance that the researcher wants to measure—a hormone, in Yalow's and Berson's case—is tagged with a radioactive isotope. Then it is mixed in solution with its naturally occurring antibody (the "immuno" part of RIA), and hormone-antibody pairs are formed. They are then added to a quantity of the patient's blood, in which there is an unknown quantity of the hormone that the researcher wants to determine. Since antibodies prefer nonradioactive versions of the hormone to radioactive ones, they gradually separate from their radioactive partners and team up with the natural hormone. A researcher then separates out all the hormone-antibody pairs (both the radioactive and the nonradioactive ones) and measures the radioactivity of the mixture. The difference in the level of radioactivity of this mixture from the radioactivity of the original sample of tagged pairs gives a measure ("assay") of how much natural hormone was in the sample of blood.

RIA Test

The RIA test is simple in principle. Three major substances are present in the reaction: antigen, radio labelled antigen and correlated specific antibody. The antibody can bind to both labelled and unlabelled antigen. It is kept constant and limited during the test. Radio labelled antigen possesses the same properties as unlabelled antigen and it is constant, too. The radiolabelled antigen is then mixed with a known amount of its antibody, resulting in formation of a labelled antigen-antibody complex, called bound antigen. When further unlabelled antigen is added to the mixture, from standards or unknown samples, this causes the new unlabelled antigen to compete with the radio labelled antigen for a fixed number of antibody or receptor binding sites, leading to more unlabelled antigen-antibody complex and reducing the ratio of antibody-bound radio labelled antigen to free radio labelled antigen. The more antigen is present, the less likely is the labelled antigen bound to the antibody, thus the amount of labelled antigen-antibody complex formed is inversely proportional to the antigen originally present in serum. For this reason, this is called a competing depression reaction.

At this point a crucial step is the complete separation between the labelled antigen-antibody complex and the remaining free labelled antigen (separation of bound from unbound labelled antigen). Refined methods had to be developed for handling this phase of the test. The antigen-antibody complexes formed are precipitated using a precipitating reagent (for example a secondary antibody) toseparate bound and free tracer.

Once the antibody-bound antigens are separated from the unbound ones, the radioactivity of both the bound and the remaining free antigen is measured using a gamma counter. With results obtained from a series of standard samples (in which the concentration of the radioactive ligand is always kept constant, but with different concentrations of the inactive ligand), a binding standard (dose-response) curve can be generated. The concentration in the unknown sample may be then read from the standard curve by interpolation.

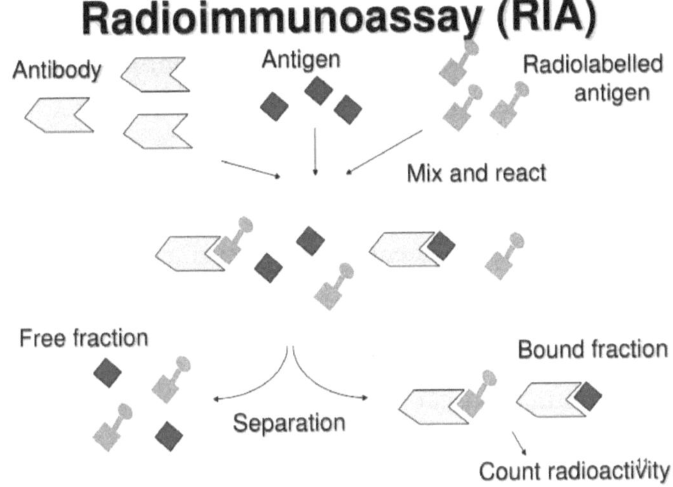

Fig. 5. Diagrammatic representation of the Radioimmunoassay (RIA) Technique.

Calibration curve

A standard curve can be constructed by plotting the percentage of antibody-bound radiolabelled antigen against known concentrations of a standardized unlabelled antigen as shown in figure. Also, the curve allows determining the unknown antigen concentration directly from the standard curve.

CALIBRATION CURVE

- From these data, a standard binding curve, like the one shown in red, can be drawn.
- The samples to be assayed (the unknowns) are run in parallel.
- After determining the ratio of bound to free antigen in each unknown, the antigen concentrations can be read directly from the standard curve.

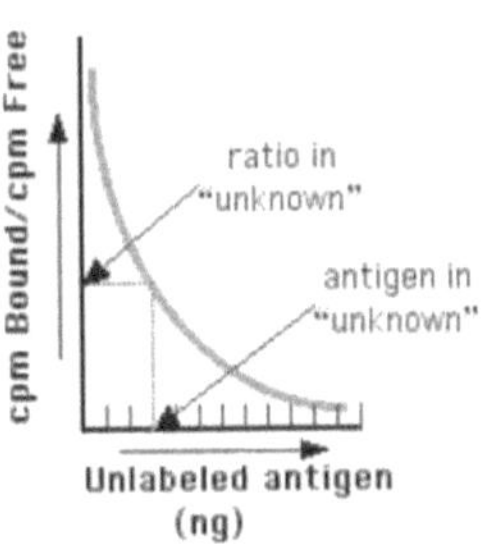

Fig.6. Plotting of a standard curve (Calibration curve) of RIA.

What are the uses of radioimmunoassay?

- It is used to determine a small number of antigens and antibodies in a particular serum.
- It is useful in quantifying of hormones, HBsAg, drugs, and other forms of viral antigens.
- It can check the concentration of picomolar and nanomolar hormones in biological fluids.
- It is used in the analysis of vitamins and other metabolite markers.
- Radioimmunoassay can diagnose any type of allergy.
- It has the ability to detect and diagnose cancer.
- In the blood bank, radioimmunoassay is used to track and screen leukaemia and hepatitis virus, which is highly contagious.
- It is used to diagnose and treat peptic ulcers.
- It plays a fundamental role in the research of neurotransmitter, a chemical in the brain.

Advantages

1. Highly sensitive so it can be used for the detection of small quantities of analyte or antigens.
2. Quantification of antigens or analytes is possible with RIA.

Limitations

1. The handling of radioisotopes requires specific safety measures. Because of this limitation, RIA has been replaced by ELISA in clinical laboratories.

Importance of RIA and its major future application

Radioimmunoassay was a historic breakthrough in science since it was the first technique that harnessed the power of radioisotopes to follow how antigens reacted with antibodies. Today, their technique is used across the sciences in screening for hepatitis in blood blanks, correcting hormone levels, and in creating the most effective dosages of drugs and antibiotics. Under her guidance, scientists were trained in RIA which began to be widely used in laboratories across the globe.

Fig.7. Rosalyn Sussman Yalow (1921–2011)

Ultimately, RIA created "an explosion of knowledge" in every aspect of medicine and was used in thousands of laboratories in the United States and abroad.

Thyroid Gland Function Tests

James Norman, MD, FACS, FACE

Endocrine Web Founder, Parathyroid Surgeon

Jun 1, 2020

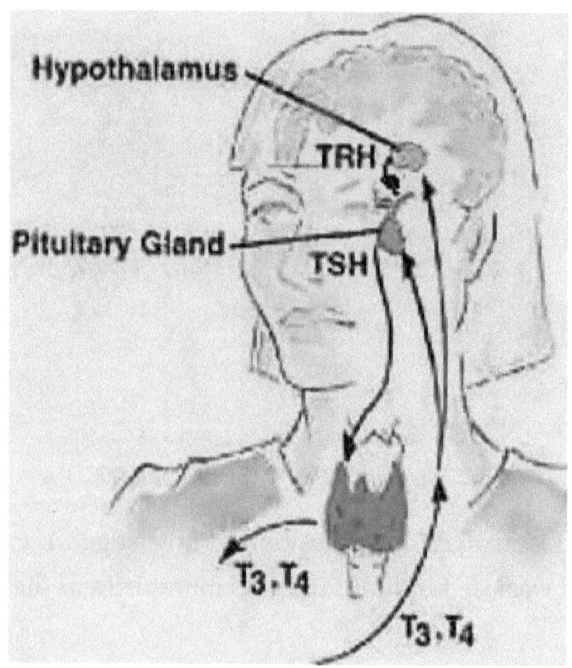

Fig. 8. Basic elements in the regulation of thyroid function.

From the overview of normal thyroid physiology, it is observed that the thyroid gland produces T4 and T3. But this production is not possible without stimulation from the pituitary gland (TSH) which in turn is also regulated by the hypothalamus's TSH Releasing Hormone. Now, with radioimmunoassay techniques it is possible to measure circulating hormones in the blood very accurately. Knowledge of this thyroid physiology is important in knowing what thyroid test or tests are needed to diagnose different diseases. No one single laboratory test is 100% accurate in diagnosing all types of thyroid disease; however, a combination of two or more tests can usually detect even the slightest abnormality of thyroid function.

For example, a low T4 level could mean a diseased thyroid gland ~OR ~a non-functioning pituitary gland which is not stimulating the thyroid to produce T4. Since the pituitary gland would normally release TSH if the T4 is low, a high TSH level would confirm that the thyroid gland (not the pituitary gland) is responsible for the hypothyroidism.

If the T4 level is low and TSH is not elevated, the pituitary gland is more likely to be the cause for the hypothyroidism. Of course, this would drastically affect the treatment since the pituitary gland also regulates the body's other glands (adrenals, ovaries, and testicles) as well as controlling growth in children and normal kidney function. Pituitary gland failure means that the other glands may also be failing and other treatment than just thyroid may be necessary. The most common cause for the pituitary gland failure is a tumour of the pituitary and this might also require surgery to remove.

Measurement of Thyroid hormones

Modern measurement of thyroid hormones is done by a new technique, radioimmunoassay (RIA), discovered by Dr. Solomon Berson and Dr. Rosalyn Yalow. Rosalyn Yalow was also awarded the 1977 Nobel Prize in Medicine for this discovery which revolutionized the study of thyroid disease as well as the entire field of Endocrinology. The technique "brought a revolution in biological and medical research," the Karolinska Institute in Sweden said in awarding Dr. Yalow, along with Andrew V. Schally, M. D., Ph. D., and Roger Guillemin, M. D., Ph. D., the Nobel Prize in 1977. (Dr. Berson would have shared the prize but he died before the award was given).

Biography of Rosalyn Sussman Yalow

Rosalyn Sussman, sometimes characterized as "Madame Curie of the Bronx," was born on July 19, 1921 in New York City, as the only daughter and second child of uneducated, lower middle-class Jewish parents, Clara and Simon Sussman. Her father, Simon Sussman, was son of a Russian immigrant, and her mother, Clara Zipper was a German immigrant. Clara Zipper, came to America from Germany at the age of four. She was a daughter of parents who never finished high school. Her father, Simon Sussman, was born on the Lower East Side of New York, the Melting Pot for Eastern European immigrants. Simon Sussman, whose education had ended at the eighth grade, and who sold paper and twine out of his small neighbourhood store, Rosalyn's motherClara Zipper Sussmanhad also dropped out of school. She was a homemaker. To earn money for the family, Clara took in piece-work sewing, and Rosalyn helped by turning collars at home for her uncle's neckwear factory. She had an elder brother named Alexander. He was solelyresponsible for the trip every week to the Public Library to exchange books already read for new ones to be read. Rosalyn came from a family of strong women. Even as a child, Rosalyn showed the same matriarchal characteristics as her elders. She was outspoken, supremely confident, and fearless. Her brother called her "**The Queen Bee**."

Yalow, in her Nobel biography, described herself as a "stubborn, determined child," with a fondness for reading and a dedication to mathematics in junior high school, which developed in seventh grade. By the age of eight, she aspired of being a scientist. She attended Walton High School, at the time an all-girls institution, where she became interested in chemistry. At Walton High School she had changed her career plans to chemistry, thanks to a talented chemistry teacher, Mr. Mondzak, whoexcited her interest in chemistry.

As a smart but poor New York City girl, Yalow attended Hunter College, a highly competitive free women's college. Her parents fought for her to study education and become a teacher like other learned young ladies of her time. But she wanted to be a physicist, so instead she became Hunter's first physics major, graduating early and with honours.

But when she went to Hunter, the college for women in New York City's college system (now the City University of New York), her interest was diverted from chemistry to physics especially by having received more encouragement from her physics professors, Prof. Herbert N. Otis, and Prof. Duane Roller than from the chemistry faculty. In the late '30's when she was in college, physics, and in particular nuclear physics, was the most exciting field in the world.

Also while in college Yalow read Eve Curie's biography of her Nobel Prize – winning mother,Marie Curie, which excited Yalow about nuclear physics, a hot new field in the late 1930s. It should be a must on the reading list of every young aspiring female scientist. In 1939 an Italian scientist, Enrico Fermigave a colloquium in January 1939 on the newly discovered nuclear fission – which has resulted not only in the terror and threat of nuclear warfare but also in the ready availability of radioisotopes for medical investigation and in hosts of other peaceful applications. Hearing the lectures, Yalowwas very excitedand more determined to pursue a career in nuclear science. Here she took up nuclear physics as her major subject. She persisted with her studies even though her parents wanted her to be a school teacher.

Yalow graduated from Hunter College Phi Beta Kappa, magna cum laude, with a BA in chemistry and physics, in 1941 with Honours and joined a business school where she did not stay for long. She was the perfect candidate for a graduate fellowship, but she was turned down by one university after another. Only one admissions office was honest enough to admit the real reason: they believed that, as a Jew and a woman, she would never get a job in the field.

After she applied to Purdue University for a graduate assistantship to study physics, the university wrote back to her professor: "She is from New York. She is Jewish. She is a woman. If you can guarantee her a job afterward, we'll give her an assistantship." No guarantee was possible, and the rejection hurt, Dr. Yalow told an interviewer. "They told me that as a woman, I'd never get into graduate school in physics," she said, "so they got me a job as a secretary at the College of Physicians and Surgeons and promised that, if I were a good girl, I would take courses there."

Yalow was well prepared for these setbacks. In college, she had been warned to take typing and steno courses so she could support herself as a secretary while going to school. It was simply an alternative way to work toward a doctorate. The Sussmans did not have the money required for their daughter's graduate tuition without some kind of financial aid. If she worked at a university, she would be permitted to take courses gratis. Rosalyn accepted a secretarial job at Columbia University and prepared to take night classes.

As I entered the last half of my senior year at Hunter in September 1940, I was offered what seemed like a good opportunity. Since I could type, another of my physics professors, Dr. Jerrold Zacharias, now at Massachusetts Institute of Technology, obtained a part time position for me as a secretary to Dr. Rudolf Schoenheimer, a leading biochemist at Columbia University's College of Physicians and Surgeons (P&S). This position was supposed to provide an entrée for me into graduate courses, via the backdoor, but I had to agree to take stenography.

In mid-February of that year, she received an offer of a teaching assistantship in physics at the University of Illinois at Urbana-Champaign with the primary reason being that World War II commenced and many men went off to war and the university decided to offer scholarships for women rather than shut down. That summer she took two tuition-free physics courses under government auspices at New York University.

In September 1941, Yalow entered the University of Illinois, becoming the only woman among the 400-member faculty of the College of Engineering, and the first woman there since 1917, according to the Dean of Faculty at the time. Yalow credited her position at the prestigious graduate school to the shortage of male candidates during World War II. Being surrounded by gifted men made her aware of a wider world in science. They recognized her talent, they encouraged her, and they supported her. They were in a position to help her succeed.

The first year in theUniversity was not easy. *"From junior high school through Hunter College, I had never had boys in my classes, except for a thermodynamics course which I took at City College at night and the two summer courses at NYU. Hunter had offered a physics major for the first time in September 1940 when I was an upper senior. As a result, my course work in physics had been minimal for a major – less than that of the other first year graduate students. Therefore, at Illinois I sat in on two undergraduate courses without credit, took three graduate courses and was a half-time assistant teaching the freshman course in physics. Like nearly all first-year teaching assistants, I had never taught before – but unlike the others I also undertook to observe in the classroom of a young instructor with an excellent reputation so that I could learn how it should be done."*

As a Jewish woman, Rosalyn Sussman was unique among her classmates when she began graduate school in physics at the University of Illinois in 1941. Three and a half years later, more quickly than anyone else in her program, she completed her Ph. D. On the first day of graduate school, she met Aaron Yalow. He had come to Illinois to start graduate study in physics.

They married on June 6, 1943. They had two children: Benjamin, a systems programmer, and Elanna, an educational psychologist. It is clear that nothing was going to stop her from achieving her goals, and that this aggressive drive affected those close to her.

A Jewish woman whose father-in-law is a rabbi, who keeps a **kosher home**, who invites her lab assistants to Passover Seders and worries about them catching colds, is not the typical image of a Nobel Prize winner. But it is the image of Rosalyn Yalow, the first woman born and educated in the United States to win a Nobel Prize in a scientific field.

N. B.:

Rabbi:

A rabbi is a Jewish religious leader, usually one who is in charge of a synagogue, one who is qualified to teach Judaism, or one who is an expert on Jewish law.

Kosher:

The word kosher, literally meaning "clean" or "pure," refers to food that has been ritually prepared or blessed so it can be eaten by religious Jews. It comes from the Hebrew word Kasher, meaning "proper" or "lawful," and became common in English in the mid-19th Century. It can be used as an adjective, for example, "kosher meat." In the mid-1920's, the word took on a more general meaning, used to refer to anything that was acceptable.

General Rules

Although the details of kashrut are extensive, the laws all derive from a few fairly simple, straightforward rules:

1. Certain animals may not be eaten at all. This restriction includes the flesh, organs, eggs, and milk of the forbidden animals. This

applies only to eating the animals. You can play football with a pig skin ball or wear pig skin gloves or shoes.

2. Of the animals that may be eaten, the birds and mammals must be killed in accordance with Jewish law.

3. All blood must be drained from meat and poultry or broiled out of it before it is eaten.

4. Certain parts of permitted animals may not be eaten.

5. Fruits and vegetables are permitted, but must be inspected for bugs (which cannot be eaten).

6. Meat (the flesh of birds and mammals) cannot be eaten with dairy. Fish, eggs, fruits, vegetables, and grains can be eaten with either meat or dairy. (According to some views, fish may not be eaten with meat).

7. Utensils (including pots and pans and other cooking surfaces) that have come into contact with meat may not be used with dairy, and vice versa. Utensils that have come into contact with non-kosher food may not be used with kosher food. This applies only where the contact occurred while the food was hot.

8. Grape products made by non-Jews may not be eaten.

9. There are a few other rules that are not universal.

What is Kosher?

The definition of kosher is usually explained as acceptable or proper. It has informally been used in the English language as that meaning. The laws of kosher food originated in the Bible, and have been observed by Jews for over 3,000 years. These laws are detailed in the Talmud and other codes of Jewish tradition. The laws of kosher go beyond the prohibition of not eating pigs. There are many intricacies involved in the basic kosher laws.

The Bible lists the basic categories that are not kosher Meat, fowl, fish, most insects, and any shellfish or reptile (Pig, camel, eagle, and catfish etc.). The animals that are permissible to eat must be slaughtered according to Jewish law. Meat and dairy items must be kept separate and not manufactured or consumed together. In order to indicate the variables of kosher and non-kosher depends on the source of the ingredients and the status of the production. Kosher certification guarantees that the food meets kosher requirements.

Sources

The guidelines for the sources of kosher and non-kosher materials originate in the Bible. Kosher food is separated into three different categories, Meat, Dairy and Pareve.

Meat

Mammals that chew their cud and have split hooves are deemed kosher. They must have both of these characteristics in order to be rendered kosher for example: cow, deer, and goat. After determining the status of the animal, they must be slaughtered by a specialist (shochet) and then koshered (soaked and salted to remove the blood) before eating. All other animals, even if they have one of these features are not considered Kosher, for example: Pig, camel, and rabbit.

Fowl

All non-kosher fowl is listed in the Bible in Deuteronomy. Fowl falls under the meat category. Examples of kosher fowl are chicken, duck, and turkey.

Of all the animals and fowls that are permitted to eat, they must be killed in accordance to Jewish law.

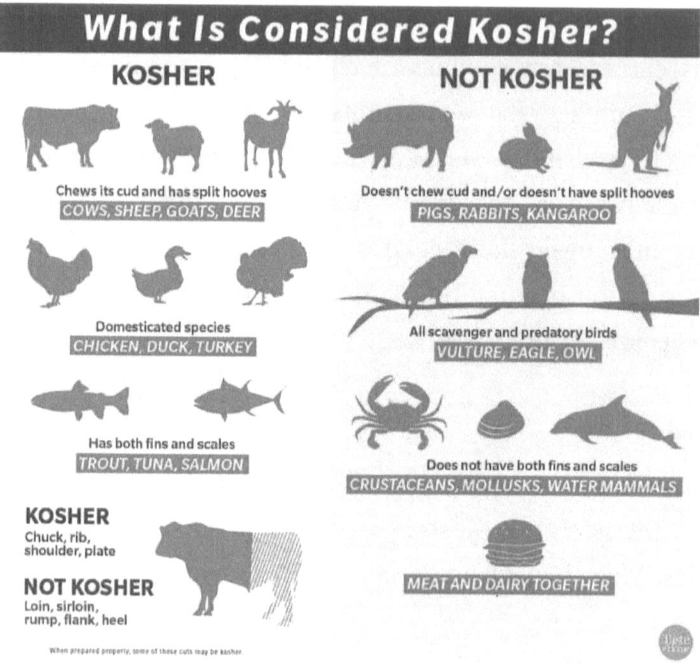

Fig. 9. Kosher and Not Kosher food items Dairy

Dairy foods must come from a kosher animal. They may not be eaten together with meat or fowl.

Pareve

Pareve foods are neither meat nor dairy. Examples are vegetables, fruit, grains they must be in their natural state to be determined as Pareve. Fish which must have fins and scales is also considered pareve. Examples of kosher fish are tuna, salmon, tilapia. All shellfish, shark, reptiles, and underwater mammals are not kosher.

Equipment

Equipment used to manufacture non-kosher ingredients may acquire a non-kosher status. Therefore, production done after a non-kosher run may render the food non-kosher even if only kosher ingredients were used. Non-kosher equipment can be restored to a kosher status by koshering the equipment. This can be done by either pouring hot water over the equipment or raising the heat on the oven depending on the equipment and what non-kosher item was used on the equipment beforehand.

Kosher Food for the Modern-Day Consumer

Kosher food must adhere to the rules listed above. Jewish foods for example knishes, latkes, kugels etc.are not kosher unless prepared in accordance to the laws of Kashrus. There are numerous rules and regulations regarding Kosher certification. In recent years, different Kashrus organizations certify foods on the food package, in order to determine their kashrus status. This is usually indicated by a symbol stating its kashrus status. For example, OU, OK, KOF-K, and star K. These organizations send emissaries to the food plants to ensure that the product compiles with the appropriate kashrus standards.

Kosher Kitchen

Is it Kosher?

Meaning "fit" in Hebrew, kosher refers to a set of Jewish dietary laws from the Bible as interpreted by rabbis in the Talmud, written commentary that began some two thousand years ago.

To Be Kosher

- An animal must both chew its cud and have a cloven (divided) hoof. Therefore, cows are kosher, but pigs are not.
- Fish must have both scales and fins. So, tuna is kosher, but lobster is not.
- Animals must be killed painlessly by a Schochet, a ritual slaughterer, and then drained of blood.
- Milk and meat cannot be cooked or eaten together.
- Dishes and utensils for dairy and meat must be kept separate.

Only a minority of American Jews follow the kosher laws, but the word has become common slang, meaning "legitimate" or "fair."

Making your Kitchen Kosher

Before a kitchen can be used for kosher foods, all traces of non-kosher must be purged, and sufficient utensils must be designated for meat, dairy and pareve.

The general rule of thumb is that the non-kosher must be removed in the same manner in which it was absorbed. A drinking glass into which one accidentally poured some cold non-kosher wine can simply be rinsed thoroughly. Cooking pots, however, would be purged by waiting 24 hours, and then cleansed with boiling water (a process known as hagalah). A skillet, on the other hand, would need to be heated directly on the fire (known as libun) or run through a cleaning cycle in a self-cleaning oven.

Some substances, such as pottery, cannot be properly purged at all. A porcelain sink, for example, cannot be made kosher, and the kosher consumer would need to take care not to wash their dishes directly in a sink that had been used for milk and meat or other non-kosher.

In addition, glass and metal utensils purchased from non-Jewish sources must be immersed in a mikvah.

Maintaining a Kosher Kitchen

Some basic rules to ensure that a kosher kitchen remains kosher, and that all the food produced therein is also kosher:

- All ingredients, without exception, must be certified kosher, or, like most fruits and vegetables, known to be kosher without certification.
- Meat and dairy must be kept strictly separate. Even the smallest drop of mixing can be extremely problematic.

- When preparing for a meat meal, all foods must be chopped, peeled, and stored with utensils designated for meat. Likewise, when preparing for a dairy meal. Parve dishes may be used for fruits, vegetables, etc., but may never be in direct contact with either meat or dairy.

- When washing dishes in a sink that is used for both meat and dairy, be sure not to place the dishes onto the surface of the sink.

- Most follow the convention that ovens and dish washers must be designated for exclusive use with meat or dairy and may not be used for both (even if not being used at the same time).

- While non-Jews may assist with most of the cooking, the fires must be turned onby a Jewish person.

Fig. 10. Kosher kitchens that prove why doubles are trendy.

Kosher Food Items

Breakfast

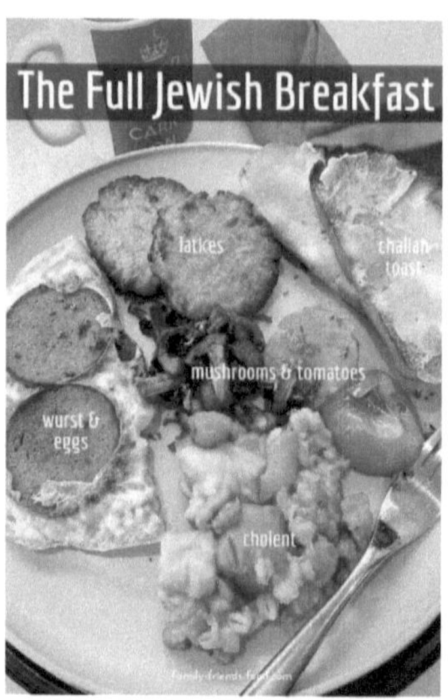

The Full Jewish Breakfast

Sheet Pan Omelette

Breakfast muffins

*Breakfast sliders
(Cheese and Sausage)*

Various Traditional Meals

Fig. 11. Various Jewish traditional dishes

Walton High School

Walton High School was a public four-year high school located in the Jerome Park neighbourhood of the Bronx borough in New York. Originally an all-girl institution, Walton became co-educational in 1977.

Fig. 12. Walton High School

History

Walton High School is named after Mary Walton, a wife of GeneralLewis Morris, a member of the Continental Congress and a signer of the Declaration of Independence and the U. S. Constitution, as well as one of the first members of New York State's Board of Regents. Mary Walton was the mother of ten children, four of whom fought in the American Revolutionary War. The Walton and the Morris families owned land in the west Bronx from the 17th until the 19th century. Mary Walton operated a "dame school", teaching little girls of the colonial period to read, write, do basic mathematics, and keep house. Mary Walton was buried next to Saint Ann's Church in the South Bronx. Mary A. Conlon, an elementary school principal of P. S. 30 (located next to Mary Walton's burial place), founded Walton as one of the first all-girl schools in New York City. TheNew York City Board of Education accredited Walton as an all-girlhigh schoolon April 19, 1923. The first graduation took place in January 1926 with 126 girls.

Located in: Young Adult Borough Centers @ Walton Campus (YABC)
Address: 2780 Reservoir Ave, The Bronx, NY 10468, United States
Phone:+1 718-364-2530
District: New York City Public Schools
Founder: Mary A. Conlon
Founded: 1923
Number of students: 1,191 (2007–2008)
Colours: White, Blue
Mascot: Wildcats
Motto: Semper Fidelis (Latin for "always faithful")

Notable alumni of Walton High School

- Bella Abzug, (1920–1998), nicknamed "Battling Bella", was a lawyer, U. S. Representative, social activist, and leader in the women's movement.

- Isabel Bigley, (1926–2006) was an American actress.

- Coko(born 1970), is an American singer-song writer best known as the lead singer of the R&B vocal trio Sisters With Voices(SWV)

- Gertrude Elion, (1918–1999) was an American biochemist and pharmacologist, who shared the 1988 Nobel Prize in Physiology or Medicine

- Oswald Feliz, is an American politician and attorney serving as a member of theNew York City Council

- Shari Lewis, (1933–1998) was an American TV legend ventriloquist, puppeteer, children's entertainer, and television show host.

- Leanne "Lelee" Lyons, (born 1973) is an American singer – songwriter and television personality. Member of the R&B vocal trioSisters With Voices(SWV)

- Penny Marshall, (1943–2018) was an American award-winning actress, director, and producer.

- Rosalyn Sussman Yalow, (1921–2011) was an American medical physicist, and a co-winner of the 1977 Nobel Prize in Physiology or Medicine.

- Anna Jacobson Schwartz, (1915–2012) was an American economist who worked at the National Bureau of Economic Research in New York City and a writer for The New York Times.

Rosalyn Yalow Charter School

About

A few years after Yalow died, in 2015, a K-5 grade charter school opened in the Bronx where she grew up and was named in her honour. The Rosalyn Yalow Charter School is a K-5 grade school in District 9 of the Bronx, which opened September 1, 2015 with 211 K-1 students. Now in our sixth year, Yalow serves 525 K-5 students. It honours Nobel Laureate Rosalyn S. Yalow (1921–2011), a physicist and the second American woman to win the Nobel Prize in Physiology or Medicine (1977). The school wrote in its mission statement, "Our hope is that Dr. Yalow's legacy will inspire a new generation of Bronx children to work hard at their education and strive for success."

Fig. 13. Rosalyn Yalow Charter School

The Rosalyn Yalow Charter School fosters a collaborative learning environment, using arts, music, and disciplined activities such as chess and fencing to engage the children and their families in the education process. The school has a longer schoolday – 9 hours – and integrates academic teaching with arts, music, chess, and fencing throughout the day (no after-school programs). Yalow Charter School is data-driven, using the NWEA and STEP assessment programs to guide Teachers, Administrators, and Board members in making professional development decisions.

Our new campus at Cardinal Hayes High School is beautiful, with amenities such as a 10,000 square foot playground as well as a large auditorium for student music programs.

The NYS Education Department named Rosalyn Yalow a 2020 Achievement Recognition School, placing Yalow in the top 13%of all public schools in New York State. In addition to strong academic programs, we will provide our students with free mental health counselling, in addition to medical, dental, and vision care at no cost to families without insurance from Montefiore's School Health Program.

Hunter College and Illinois University (where Rosalyn Sussman Yalow Studied)

Yalow graduated magna cum laude from Hunter College in New York, earning the first physics degree awarded by the college. In an era when few women pursued careers in science, she persisted in applying to graduate schools and was offered a teaching assistantship at the University of Illinois College of Engineering, where she was the only woman among 400 teaching fellows and faculty members in 1941. Her thesis director was Maurice Goldhaber, who later became director of Brookhaven National Laboratories. While at Illinois, Yalow became proficient at making and using instruments for measuring radioactive substances. Those skills would prove crucial to her later research career.

Yalow graduated with a doctorate in nuclear physics from Illinois in 1945. A native New Yorker, she returned home to work briefly as an engineer and then took a position teaching physics at

Hunter College. Keen to do research, however, she volunteered at what is now the James J. Peters Veterans Affairs Medical Centre. There, she developed a radioisotope unit and collaborated with physicians on research.

Hunter College

Fig. 14. Logo of Hunter College

Thomas Hunter

Order: 1st

Dates: 1870–1906

Compelled to leave Ireland because he was "a republican and revolutionist," Thomas Hunter arrived in New York in 1850 and, for lack of other employment, soon found himself teaching drawing, then reading, writing, and arithmetic at "No. 35," a public grammar school for boys. He had found his metier; historians of American education rank his work, both practical and theoretical, with that of John Dewey. Rising swiftly in his now chosen profession, he soon became the school's principal, then also founder and principal of the first free evening high school in America.

He became president of the newly established "Female Normal and High School" on Fourth Street and Broadway when it opened on St. Valentine's Day in 1870. The original Park Avenue building, for which he himself drew the plans, opened in September 1873. This first publicly supported college for women in America took on the name of its founder in 1914.

In Brief

Hunter College of the City University of New York was founded in 1870 as a public, tuition-free secondary and teacher-training school for women that admitted students solely on the basis of academic merit, at a time when many institutions of higher education were implementing policies of selective admissions designed specifically to deflect disadvantaged students. As such, African American, Catholic, and Jewish women attended Hunter in disproportionate numbers, and Hunter's student body differed significantly from that of other women's colleges in America. Hunter educated scores of intellectually gifted and professionally talented women, including Nobel prize winners, politicians, authors, and pageant winners. In recent years, Hunter's student population has continued to reflect the demographics of New York City, though it is now coeducational and charges tuition.

Hunter College Today

In recent years, Hunter's student population has continued to reflect the demographics of New York City. Now a senior college of the City University of New York, offering a vast array of undergraduate, graduate, and certificate programs, Hunter is coeducational, charges tuition, and attracts an extraordinarily diverse student body. After a decline in Jewish enrolments in the

1970s and 1980s, the college is again witnessing an upsurge as recent immigrants and refugees from the former Soviet bloc countries apply for admission. By becoming Hunter students, they are joining a long list of distinguished alumni, including Nobel Prize winners Rosalyn Sussman Yalow and Gertrude Belle Elion, author Bel Kaufman, politician Bella Abzug, consumer advocate and former Miss America Bess Myerson, and several presidents of Hadassah. These alumni demonstrate the tradition that placed Jewish students in the forefront of the drive for education.

Fig. 15. Hunter College, New York City

Overview

Relevant Information about Hunter College

CUNY – Hunter College is a public institution that was founded in 1870. It has a total undergraduate enrolment of 18,152 (fall 2021), and the setting is Urban. It utilizes a semester-based academic calendar. CUNY-Hunter College's ranking in the 2022–2023 edition of Best Colleges is Regional Universities North, #21. Its in-state tuition and fees are $7,380; out-of-state tuition and fees are $19,050.

Students at Hunter College, a City University of New York institution, attend class in Manhattan. Many students commute after class, though, as only a small percentage of students live in university housing. The college has a large arts program and grants degrees in art, dance, film, music, and theatre. The Hunter College Hawks compete in the NCAA's Division III.

Hunter College runs a variety of research centres and institutes, including the Centre for Puerto Rican Studies, or Centro; the Centre for Community and Urban Health; and the CUNY Institute for Sustainable Cities. The school also offers an International English Language Institute for non-native speakers that has courses during the day, in the evenings and on weekends.

Notable Alumni of Hunter College

Notable alumni of Hunter College include Gertrude Elion and Rosalyn Yalow, both winners of the Nobel Prize in medicine, and stand-up comedian Natasha Leggero.

The List of Hunter College Alumni

Nobel laureates

- Gertrude B. Elion – 1988, Medicine
- Rosalyn Sussman Yalow – 1977, Medicine

Pulitzer Prize winners

- Holland Cotter – art critic
- Emily Grenauer – art critic
- Ada Louise Huxtable – architecture critic

- Liu Heung Sheng– photographer
- James Wright– poet
- National Medal of Science winners
- Mildred Cohn – 1982, Biological Sciences
- Mildred Dresselhaus – Engineering Sciences
- Gertrude B. Elion

Presidential Medal of Freedom winners

- Antonia Pantoja– activist

Science, technology, medicine, and mathematics

- Patricia Bath– ophthalmologist
- Marjorie Clarke – environmental scientist
- Mildred Cohn-National Medal of Science winner

Mary P. Dolciani – mathematician

- Elsie Giorgi– physician
- Erich Jarvis– neurologist
- Esther Lederberg – pioneer of bacterial genetics
- Lena Levine – psychiatrist, gynaecologist, pioneer of marriage counselling and birth control
- Beatrice Mintz – pioneer of mammalian transgenesis
- Arlie Petters – pioneer of gravitational lensing
- Mina Rees – mathematician, President of the American Association for the Advancement of Science
- Gillian Reynolds 1988 – third African American woman to earn a Ph. D. in Physics fromM. I. T.
- Ruth Teitelbaum-ENIAC programmer
- Rosalyn Sussman Yalow – Nobel prize winner in Medicine

Business and economics

- Gerard Cafesjian – owner of West Publishing Corporation (now part of Thomson Corporation)
- Alan S. Chartock – president and CEO of WAMC
- Leon Cooperman – billionaire hedge fund manager
- Robert A. Daly-CEO of Warner Bros. and the Los Angeles Dodgers
- Mollie Orshansky – developer of the Orshansky Poverty Thresholds, the main poverty measure in the US
- Sylvia Field Porter – economist and journalist
- Melvin T. Tukman – co-founder and president of Tukman Grossman Capital Management, an investment firm.
- Law and politics

Members of Congress

- Bella Abzug – Congresswoman, 1971–1977
- Eliot L. Engel – Congressman, 1989–present
- Edna F. Kelly – Congresswoman, 1949–1969

State figures

- Teresa Patterson Hughes – California State Senator
- Roger Manno – Maryland House of Delegates

City figures

- Tony Avella – New York City councilman, 2009 candidate for mayor
- Adolfo Carrión Jr. – Bronx borough president
- Tom Murphy – mayor of Pittsburgh
- John Timoney – Miami chief of police

Lawyers

- Floria Lasky – prominent theatre lawyer
- Soia Mentschikoff – chief developer of the Uniform Commercial Code and first woman to teach at Harvard Law School

Activists

- Norma Becker – anti-war activist
- Madeleine Cosman – health care and immigration advocate
- Alexander Dvorkin – anti-cult activist
- Theodora Lacey – civil rights activist
- Audre Lorde – activist, writer, poet
- Pauli Murray – activist, lawyer, priest, and author
- Antonia Pantoja – activist, Presidential Medal of Freedom winner
- Mamphela Ramphele-Rockefeller Foundation trustee, anti-apartheid activist
- Sandra Schnur – pioneer of disability rights
- Judith Vladeck – labour lawyer and civil rights advocate

Journalism and news

- Mohamad Bazzi– journalist
- Richard Cohen-Washington Postcolumnist
- Corine Hegland – journalist

Jack Newfield – muckraking journalist

- Shimon Prokupecz-CNNreporter
- Daniel Seaman – Israeli politician; expert on the Arab-Israeli conflict

Literature

- Grace Andreacchi– writer
- Maurice Berger – cultural critic

- Peter Carey– writer
- Colin Channer– writer
- Helen Gray Cone– poet
- Lucy Dawidowicz – author
- Martin Greif – writer, publisher
- Kaitlyn Greenidge – writer
- Evan Hunter – author and screenwriter
- Ada Louise Huxtable – writer,Pulitzer Prize-winning architectural critic
- Colette Inez – poet, academic
- Swati Khurana – writer
- Malka Lee – poet
- Audre Lorde – poet, essayist
- Paule Marshall – author,MacArthur Fellow"genius grant,"Dos Passos Prize for Literature
- Barbara McMartin – environmental writer
- Melissa Plaut – writer
- Sylvia Field Porter – economist, journalist
- Sonia Sanchez – poet
- Augusta Huiell Seaman – writer
- Sadia Shephard – writer
- Gary Shteyngart – author
- René Taupin – writer
- Ned Vizzini – writer
- Joan Wolf – writer of romance novels
- James Wright – poet
- Ricky Anne Loew-Beer – Author, Artist & Photographer (married to fashion designer Ralph Lauren)

Film, theatre, and television

- Ellen Barkin – actress
- Lewis Beale – film critic
- Ed Burns – actor, director
- Eva Condon – Broadway actress
- Judith Crist – film critic
- Ruby Dee – actress
- Vin Diesel – actor
- Hugh Downs – broadcaster,20/20 and The Today Show anchor
- Tina Howe – Tony-nominated playwright
- Chad Hunt – director
- Richard Jeni – comedian
- Suzanne Kaaren – actress
- Ephraim Katz – author of The Film Encyclopedia
- Evelyn Lear – opera singer
- Natasha Leggero – actress and comic
- Maitland McDonagh – film critic
- Daniel Mulloy – screenwriter and film director
- Julianne Nicholson – actress
- Rhea Perlman – actress
- Dascha Polanco – actress
- Esther Rolle – actress
- Regina Resnik – opera singer
- Al Santos – actor
- Elliot Tiber – screenwriter who "saved"Woodstock Festival
- Dreya Weber– producer

Art, architecture, and engineering

- Robert Altman-Rolling Stone photo journalist
- Firelei Báez – artist
- Maurice Berger – art critic and historian
- Jack Coggins – illustrator
- Francisco Costa – creative director of Calvin Klein Collection
- Jules de Balincourt – artist
- Jacqueline Donachie – artist
- Mildred Dresselhaus – engineer
- Echo Eggebrecht – painter
- Arthur Elgort – photographer for Vogue magazine
- Gabriele Evertz – abstract artist
- Denise Green – painter
- Ada Louise Huxtable – architecture critic
- Mel Kendrick – artist
- Kathleen Kucka – painter
- Terrance Lindall – artist
- Robert Morris – sculptor
- Doug Ohlson – abstract artist
- Lucy Olcott – art historian and dealer
- Mitchell Silver – urban planner
- Jeff Sonhouse – (MFA 2001), painter
- Louis A. Waldman – art historian
- Dan Walsh – painter
- Brian Wood-visual artist

Music

- David Sampson – composer
- Ashley Choi – lead singer of the bandLadies' Code

Military

- Thomas P. Noonan, Jr.-Medal of Honorrecipient

Education

- Robert Davila – ninth president of Gallaudet University
- Howard McParlin Davis – prominent art history professor
- John Taylor Gatto – author of seminal books on education
- Francis Kilcoyne(died 1985) – President of Brooklyn College
- Soia Mentschikoff – chief developer of theUniform Commercial Codeand first woman to teach at Harvard University
- Burton Pike – professor Emeritus,Comparative Literature,CUNY Graduate Centre
- Jennifer Raab – president ofHunter College
- Henning Rübsam – choreographer, dance historianThe Juilliard School
- Kay Toliver – mathematics educator

Fictional alumni

- Chad Kroski
- Harry "Parry" Sagan from
- The Fisher King
- Daniel Bae fromThe Sun Is Also a Star
- Non-graduating attendees
- Harry Connick, Jr – musician
- Bobby Darin – musician
- Nikolai Fraiture – bassist,The Strokes
- April Lee Hernández – actress
- Grace Paley – writer
- Nick Valensi – guitarist, The Strokes
- Mitski – musician

Faculty

- Meena Alexander – poet and author
- James Aronson – journalist, founder of the National Guardian
- John Avlon – author, speech writer forRudy Giuliani
- Jacqueline Barton – chemist
- William Baziotes – painter
- Harry Binswanger – philosopher
- Gertrude Blanch – pioneer of numerical analysis and computation
- Robert A. Brady – economist
- José Ferrer Canales – writer, activist
- Rosario Candela – influential architect
- Peter Carey – novelist
- Tina Chang – poet
- John Henrik Clarke – historian
- Buck Clayton – musician
- Daniel I. A. Cohen – mathematician and computer scientist
- Janet Cox-Rearick – art historian
- Noah Creshevsky – composer
- Susan Crile – painter
- Emil Draitser – author
- Cora DuBois – cultural anthropologist
- Stuart Ewen
- Norman Finkelstein – political scientist
- Mary Flanagan
- Helen Frankenthaler – artist
- Bertram Myron Gross – author of the Humphrey-Hawkins Full Employment Act
- John Hollander – poet, literary critic

- Seymour Itzkoff – researcher
- George E. Kimball – pioneer of operations research algorithms
- Dong Kingman – artist
- Lyman Kipp – sculptor
- Rosalind E. Krauss – art critic
- Reiner Leist – photographer
- Nancy Milford – author
- Paul Moravec – composer
- Robert Motherwell – artist
- Leonard Peikoff – philosopher, founder of the Ayn Rand Institute
- Mina Rees – mathematician
- Richard Reeves – political author
- Ruth Sager – geneticist
- Carolee Schneemann – artist
- Blake Schwarzenbach – musician
- Michael Shernoff – specialist in gay community mental health
- Tony Smith – sculptor
- Harry Edward Stinson – sculptor
- John Kennedy Toole – author
- Lionel Trilling – literary critic
- Nydia Velázquez – U. S. Congresswoman, New York, 1993–present
- Alice von Hildebrand – philosopher and author
- Robert C. Weaver – first U. S. Secretary of Housing and Urban Development
- Blanche Colton Williams, professor of English literature and head of the English department
- Nari Ward, professor of combined media

Administration

- David A. Caputo – president of Hunter College; president of Pace University
- Paul LeClerc – president of Hunter College; president and CEO of New York Public Library
- Michael P. Riccards – political scientist; author; executive director of the Hall Institute for Public Policy
- Donna Shalala-U. S. Secretary of Health and Human Services; 10th president of Hunter College; president of University of Miami

University of Illinois

Fig. 16. University of Illinois Urbana-Champaign

University of Illinois, is the Centre of higher education in Illinois, U. S. It consists of three campuses, the main campus in the twin cities Champaign and Urbana and additional campuses in Chicago and Springfield.

The University of Illinois Urbana-Champaign (U of I , Illinois, University of Illinois, or UIUC) is a public land-grant research university in Illinois in the twin cities of Champaign and Urbana. It is the flagship institution of the University of Illinois system and was founded in 1867. Enrolling over 56,000 undergraduate and graduate students, the University of Illinois is one of the largest public universities by enrolment in the country.

The University of Illinois Urbana-Champaign is a member of the **Association of American Universities** and is **classified** among "R1: Doctoral Universities – Very high research activity"

As of September 2022 , the alumni, faculty members, or researchers of the university include 30 Nobel laureates, 27 **Pulitzer Prize** winners, two Fields medallists, and two **Turing Award** winners. Illinois athletic teams compete in **Division I** of the **NCAA** and are collectively known as the **Fighting Illini**. They are members of the **Big Ten Conference** and have won the **second-most conference titles. Illinois Fighting Illini football** won the **Rose Bowl Game** in 1947, 1952, 1964 and a total of five national championships. Illinois athletes have won 29 medals in **Olympic events**.

U. S. News & World Report Rankings

The 2022–**23** U. S. News & World Report's America's Best Colleges rankings rated Illinois as the number **13** Public University and the number **41** National University.

Fig. 17. Logo of the University of Illinois

*Fig. 18. The **Alma Mater**, a bronze statue by sculptor Lorado Taft, is a beloved symbol of the University of Illinois Urbana-Champaign*

Nobel Laureates – Alumni of Illinois University

Nobel Laureates & Pulitzer Prize Winners

Edward Doisy

(1892–1986) shared the Nobel Prize in medicine and physiology in 1943. Doisy discovered the chemical nature of vitamin K. His work involved synthesis, isolation, and characterization of the K vitamins. Doisy received two U of I degrees: a Bachelor of Arts (1914) and a Master of Science (1916).

Vincent Du Vigneaud

(1901–1978) won the Nobel Prize in chemistry in 1955 for his work on "biochemically important sulphur compounds, especially for achieving the first synthesis of a polypeptide hormone." Du Vigneaud received a Bachelor of Science (1923) and a Master of Science (1924) from the U of I. He served on the University faculty from 1929 to 1932.

Robert Holley

(1922–1993) won the Nobel Prize in medicine and physiology in 1968 for his work determining the precise structure of nucleic acids. He received a Bachelor of Arts in chemistry from the University of Illinois in 1942.

Jack S. Kilby

(1923–2005) shared the 2000 Nobel Prize in physics for his part in the invention and development of the integrated circuit, the microchip. Kilby received a Bachelor of Science from the University of Illinois in 1947.

Edwin Krebs

(1918–2009) shared the 1992 Nobel Prize in medicine and physiology with Edmond Fischer for their discoveries in the 1950s concerning reversible protein phosphorylation. Krebs was awarded a U of I Bachelor of Arts degree in 1940.

Polykarp Kusch

(1911–1993) shared the 1955 Nobel Prize in physics for his work toward precise measurement of the magnetic moment of the electron. Kusch received a Master of Science (1933) and a Ph. D. (1936) from the U of I.

John Robert Schrieffer

(1931–) shared the 1972 Nobel Prize in physics with faculty member John Bardeen and postdoctoral fellow Leon Cooper for their work at the U of I on the theory of super conductivity. Schrieffer received a Master of Science in 1954 and a Ph. D. in 1957 from the University and served on the physics faculty from 1959 to 1962.

Phillip A. Sharp

(1944–) shared the 1993 Nobel Prize in medicine and physiology for the discovery of split genes, which proved that genes can be composed of several separate segments. Sharp received a Ph. D. in chemistry from the U of I in 1969.

Hamilton Smith

(1931–) shared the 1978 Nobel Prize in medicine and physiology for "the discovery of restriction enzymes and their application to problems of molecular genetics." Smith graduated from University High School in 1948 and attended the U of I from 1948 to 1950.

Wendell Stanley

(1904–1971) shared the 1946 Nobel Prize in chemistry for contributions to the preparation of enzymes and virus proteins in pure form. Stanley received two U of I degrees: a Master of Science (1927) and a Ph. D. (1929).

Rosalyn Sussman Yalow.

(1921–2011) shared the 1977 Nobel Prize in medicine and physiology for the discovery and development of radioimmunoassay, a technique that employs radioactive isotopes to detect and measure the levels of insulin and hormones in the blood and in body tissues. Yalow was the second woman to win the Nobel Prize in medicine. Yalow holds two U of I degrees: a Master of Science (1942) and a Ph. D. (1945).

Nobel Laureates – Faculty

John Bardeen

(1908–1991) won the Nobel Prize in physics in 1956 and 1972, the only person to have won the physics prize twice. He shared the 1956 prize with W. H. Brattain and W. Shockley for research on semiconductors and the invention of the transistor at Bell Labs, and the 1972 prize with L. N. Cooper and J. R. Schrieffer for the theory of superconductivity, developed at the U of I. Bardeen served on the University's faculty from 1951 until his death in 1991.

Leon N Cooper

(1930–) shared the 1972 Nobel Prize in Physics with faculty member John Bardeen and alumnus John R. Schrieffer for their development of the theory of superconductivity, usually called the BCS-theory. He was a research associate at the U of I from 1955 to 1957.

Elias Corey

(1928–) won the Nobel Prize in chemistry in 1990 for his "development of the theory and methodology of organic synthesis." Corey served on the faculty in the Department of Chemistry at the University from 1951 to 1959.

Vincent Du Vigneaud

(1901–1978) won the Nobel Prize in chemistry in 1955 for his work on "biochemically important sulphur compounds, especially for achieving the first synthesis of a polypeptide hormone." Du Vigneaud received a Bachelor of Science (1923) and a Master of Science (1924) from the U of I. He served on the University faculty from 1929 to 1932.

Murray Gell-Mann

(1929–) won the Nobel Prize in Physics in 1969 for "his contributions and discoveries concerning the classification of elementary particles and their interactions." Gell-Mann was a postdoctoral research associate in 1951 and a visiting research professor from 1952–1953.

Leonid Hurwicz

(1917–2008) shared the Nobel Prize in economics in 2007 with Eric S. Maskin and Roger B. Myerson for "having laid the foundations of mechanism design theory." He served as a faculty member at the University of Illinois Department of Economics from 1949–1951.

Paul C. Lauterbur

(1929–2007) shared the Nobel Prize in physiology or medicine in 2003 with Sir Peter Mansfield for "seminal discoveries concerning the use of magnetic resonance to visualize different structures." Lauterbur was among the first scientists to use nuclear magnetic resonance in the studies of molecules, solutions, and solids. Lauterbur joined the U of I faculty in 1985.

Anthony J. Leggett

(1938–) shared the 2003 Nobel Prize in physics with Alexei A. Abrikosov and Vitaly L. Ginzburg for "pioneering contributions to the theory of superconductors and super fluids." Leggett formulated the decisive theory explaining how atoms interact and are ordered in the super fluid state. Leggett joined the U of I faculty in 1983.

Salvador Luria

(1912–1991) won the Nobel Prize in medicine and physiology in 1969 with Max Delbruck and Alfred Hershey for discoveries concerning the replication mechanism and the genetic structure of viruses. He served as a professor of bacteriology at the University from 1950 to 1959.

Sir Peter Mansfield

(1933–) shared the 2003 Nobel Prize in Medicine with faculty member Paul C. Lauterbur for "seminal discoveries concerning the use of magnetic resonance to visualize different structures." Mansfield was a research associate in the U of I department of physics from 1962 to 1964.

Rudolph Marcus

(1923–) won the Nobel Prize in chemistry in 1992 for contributions to the theory of how electrons are transferred between molecules—work that helps explain such phenomena as rust and how plants draw nourishment from light. He served as a faculty member in the U of I Department of Chemistry from 1964 to 1978 and completed much of his prize-winning research at the University.

Franco Modigliani

(1918–2003) won the Nobel Prize in economics in 1985 for two major theories: one on personal finance and one on corporate finance. He served as a faculty member in the U of I Department of Economics from 1948 to 1952.

Alvin Roth

(1951 –) shared the 2012 Nobel Memorial Prize in Economic Science for his work in market design and matching theory, which relate to how people and companies find and select one another in everything from marriage to school choice to jobs to organ donations. Roth was a member of the business faculty at Illinois from 1975–1982.

John Robert Schrieffer

(1931–) shared the 1972 Nobel Prize in physics with faculty member John Bardeen and postdoctoral fellow Leon Cooper for their work at the U of I on the theory of superconductivity. Schrieffer received a Master of Science in 1954 and a Ph. D. in 1957 from the University and served on the physics faculty from 1959 to 1962.

2007 Intergovernmental Panel on Climate Change

The 2007 Nobel Peace Prize was awarded jointly to Al Gore and to the Intergovernmental Panel on Climate Change (IPCC) for their efforts in building and disseminating greater knowledge about man-made climate change, and to lay the foundations for the measures needed to counteract that change. Eight faculty members and research scientists on the University of Illinois at Urbana-Champaign served on the IPCC and were acknowledged by the organization for their contributions to the Nobel-earning work.

Donald Wuebbles and Michael Schlesinger were recognized by special certificate by the IPCC for their leadership roles in the work.

University of Illinois at Urbana-Champaign Team

- Natalia Andronova, Adjunct Professor, Department of Atmospheric Sciences
- William Chapman, Research Scientist, Department of Atmospheric Sciences
- Katharine Hayhoe, Adjunct Research Scientist, Department of Atmospheric Sciences
- Atul Jain, Professor, Department of Atmospheric Sciences
- Stephen Long, Professor, Department of Crop Sciences
- Ken Patten, Research Scientist, Department of Atmospheric Sciences
- Michael Schlesinger, Professor, Department of Atmospheric Sciences
- John Walsh, Professor Emeritus, Department of Atmospheric Sciences
- Donald Wuebbles, Professor, Department of Atmospheric Sciences.

Nobel Laureates – University Laboratory High School Graduates

Philip Anderson

(1923–) won the Nobel Prize in physics in 1977. He shared the prize with John Van Vleck and Nevill Mott for their "fundamental theoretic investigation of the electronic structure of magnetic and disordered systems." Anderson graduated from University High School in 1940.

Hamilton Smith

(1931–) shared the 1978 Nobel Prize in medicine and physiology for "the discovery of restriction enzymes and their application to problems of molecular genetics." Smith graduated from University High School in 1948 and attended the U of I from 1948 to 1950.

James Tobin

(1918–2002) won the Nobel Prize in economics in 1981. Tobin's work provided "a basis for understanding how subjects actually behave when they acquire different assets and incur debts" by his statement of the "portfolio selection theory" of investment. Tobin graduated from University High School in 1935.

Pulitzer Prize Winners – Alumni

Leonora LaPeter Anton

(1964–) received a 2016 Pulitzer Prize for Investigative Reporting as part of a team with the Tampa Bay Times that reported on conditions in Florida's state-funded mental hospitals. Anton earned a 1986 degree in journalism.

Barry Bearak

(1949–) received the 2002 Pulitzer Prize in International Reporting for his coverage of daily life in war-ravaged Afghanistan. Bearak pursued graduate studies in journalism at the University of Illinois and earned his Master of Science in 1974.

Michael Colgrass

(1932–) won the 1978 Pulitzer Prize in Music for his piece, Deja Vu for Percussion Quartet and Orchestra, which was commissioned and premiered by the New York Philharmonic. He received his University of Illinois Bachelor of Music degree in 1956.

George Crumb

(1929–) received the 1968 Pulitzer Prize in Music for Echoes of Time and the River, commissioned to celebrate the 75th anniversary of the University of Chicago. Crumb received his University of Illinois Master of Music degree in 1952.

David Herbert Donald

(1920–2009) has twice won the Pulitzer Prize in Biography: in 1961 for Charles Sumner and the Coming of the Civil War and in 1988 for Look Homeward: A Life of Thomas Wolfe. Donald pursued graduate studies in history at the University of Illinois, receiving a Master of Arts in 1942 and a Ph. D. in 1946.

Roger Ebert

(1942–2013) won the first-ever Pulitzer Prize in Criticism in 1975 for his work as film critic for the Chicago Sun-Times. Ebert graduated from the University of Illinois with a Bachelor of Science in 1964.

Roy J. Harris

(1902–1980) shared the 1950 Pulitzer Prize in Public Service with fellow University of Illinois alumnus George Thiem. Their work exposed the presence of 37 Illinois newspapermen on an Illinois state payroll. Harris received a University of Illinois Bachelor of Arts in 1925.

Beth Henley

(1952–) won the 1981 Pulitzer Prize in Drama for her play Crimes of the Heart. Henley pursued graduate studies in theatre at the University of Illinois in the 1970s.

Hugh F. Hough

(1924–1986) shared the 1974 Pulitzer Prize for Local General Spot News Reporting with fellow University of Illinois alumnus Arthur M. Petacque for uncovering new evidence that led to the reopening of efforts to solve the 1966 murder case of Illinois Sen. Charles Percy's daughter. Hough received a University of Illinois Bachelor of Science in 1951.

Glenn Howatt

(1957–) shared in the 2013 Pulitzer Prize for Local Reporting for a series of reports on a spike in infant deaths in Minneapolis day-cares that led to legislative action strengthening regulations. He earned two master's degrees from Illinois. One in geography in 1982 and the second in journalism in 1986.

Paul Ingrassia

(1950–) shared the 1993 Pulitzer Prize for Beat Reporting for coverage of management turmoil at General Motors Corp. He earned a Bachelor of Science degree from the University in 1972.

Monroe Karmin

(1929–1999) shared the 1967 Pulitzer Prize for National Reporting for his part in exposing the connection between U. S. crime and gambling in the Bahamas. Karmin received a University of Illinois Bachelor of Science in 1950.

John J. Kim

(1974–) shared the 2011 Pulitzer Prize for Local Reporting (Chicago Sun-Times) for his photography in an immersive documentation of violence in Chicago neighbourhoods, probing the lives of victims, criminals, and detectives as a widespread code of silence impedes solutions. He earned a Bachelor of Science in advertising from the U. of I. in 1997.

Nathaniel Lash

(1992–) was the data reporter with the Tampa Bay Times team that received a 2014 Pulitzer Prize for Local Reporting for its series on the Pinellas County Schools. Lash earned his journalism degree in 2014.

Eli Murray

(1993–) shared the Pulitzer Prize for Investigative Reporting in 2022 for his work with the Tampa Bay Times in investigating toxic hazards at a Florida battery recycling plant. Murray earned a bachelor's degree in 2015 from the University of Illinois Urbana-Champaign. As a student, he received the Glenn Hanson Scholarship in Visual Communications from the College of Media.

Allan Nevins

(1890–1971) received the Pulitzer Prize in Biography twice: in 1933 for Grover Cleveland and in 1937 for Hamilton Fish. Nevins earned his Bachelor of Arts in 1912 and his Master of Arts in 1913, both from the University of Illinois.

Arthur M. Petacque

(1924–2001) shared the 1974 Pulitzer Prize for Local General Spot News Reporting with fellow University of Illinois alumnus Hugh Hough. Their work in uncovering new evidence led to a reopening the 1966 murder case of Valerie Percy. Petacque attended the University of Illinois in the 1940s.

Richard Powers

(1957–) received the 2019 Pulitzer Prize in Fiction for his novel "The Over story." He earned a master's in English/rhetoric in 1979 from the University of Illinois at Urbana-Champaign. Powers joined the Illinois faculty in 1992 and retired in 2012.

James B. Reston

(1909–1995) received the Pulitzer Prize for National Reporting in 1945 and 1957 as a reporter for the New York Times. He earned a Bachelor of Science in 1932.

Robert Lewis Taylor

(1910–1998) won the 1959 Pulitzer Prize in Fiction for his book The Travails of Jaimie McPheeters. He graduated with a Bachelor of Arts from the University in 1933.

George Thiem

(1897–1987) shared the 1950 Pulitzer Prize for Public Service with fellow University of Illinois alumnus Roy J. Harris for his part in exposing the presence of 37 Illinois newspaper men on an Illinois state payroll. Thiem earned a University of Illinois Bachelor of Science in 1921.

Carl Van Doren

(1885–1950) won the 1939 Pulitzer Prize in Biography for his book Benjamin Franklin. He graduated from the University in 1907 with a Bachelor of Arts.

Mark Van Doren

(1894–1972) received the 1940 Pulitzer Prize in Poetry for his work Collected Poems, 1922–1938. He received a University of Illinois Bachelor of Arts in 1914.

Julie Westfall

(1980 –) shared in 2016 Pulitzer Prize for Breaking News Reporting with staff of the Los Angeles Times for coverage of the San Bernadino terrorist attack. Westfall is a 2002 journalism graduate.

Abe Zaidan

(1931-) shared the 1971 Pulitzer Prize for Local Reporting as a member of the staff of the Akron (Ohio) Beacon Journal. The paper was honoured for its coverage of the Kent State University tragedy on May 4, 1970. He received a U. of I. Bachelor of Science in 1953.

Pulitzer Prize Winners – Faculty

Bill Gaines (Emeritus)

(1933–) shared in two Pulitzer Prizes in Investigative Reporting (1976 and 1988). Gaines joined the University of Illinois faculty in 2001 and was the John S. and James L. Knight Foundation Chair in Investigative and Enterprise Journalism until his retirement.

Leon Dash

(1944–) shared the 1995 Pulitzer Prize in Explanatory Journalism for his work on a family's struggle with poverty, illiteracy, crime, and drug abuse in Washington, D. C. Dash became a University of Illinois faculty member in 1998 and is a Swanlund Chair and professor of journalism and Afro-American Studies.

Richard Powers (Emeritus)

(1957 –) received the 2019 Pulitzer Prize in Fiction for his novel "The Over story." He earned a master's in English/rhetoric in 1979 from the University of Illinois at Urbana-Champaign. Powers joined the Illinois faculty in 1992 and retired in 2012.

Pulitzer Prize Winners – University Laboratory High School

George F. Will

(1941–) won the 1977 Pulitzer Prize for Commentary for his work as a syndicated columnist. He graduated from University High School in 1958.

Illinois Physics alumna and Nobel laureate Rosalyn Sussman Yalow (1921–2011)

1945 Rosalyn Yalow earns a Ph. D. in physics—the second woman to receive that degree at UIUC.

1959 Yalow and Dr. Solomon A. Berson discover radioimmunoassay (RIA), a technique which measure antibodies using radioactive material.

1977 Yalow becomes the first American woman to receive the Nobel Prize in Physiology or Medicine.

1993 Yalow receives the National Medal of Science and is inducted into the National Women's Hall of Fame.

2021 Centennial of Yalow's birth: the Heising-Simons Foundation generously donates funds creating a Rosalyn Sussman Yalow Professorship in Physics at UIUC.

2022 Investiture of Nadya Mason as the inaugural Rosalyn Sussman Yalow Professor in Physics is held on May 5th.

Rosalyn Sussman Yalow

(1921–2011) shared the 1977 Nobel Prize in medicine and physiology for the discovery and development of radioimmunoassay, a technique that employs radioactive isotopes to detect and measure the levels of insulin and hormones in the blood and in body tissues. Yalow was the second woman to win the Nobel Prize in medicine. Yalow holds two U of I degrees: a Master of Science (1942) and a Ph. D. (1945).

Fig. 19. Rosalyn Yalow with Aaron Yalow.

Fig. 20. (From left to right) Benjamin Yalow, Aaron Yalow, Rosalyn Yalow, and Elanna Yalow in 1977.

Research Life

Yalow was also juggling research work and motherhood during the early years of her career. The young mother went back to her laboratory a week after the birth of her son, bringing her baby along. She continued her lab work while nursing and caring for her baby, managing it all on very little sleep. With the birth of her second child, Yalow did exactly the same – she always tried to be present for her children. She continued to work hard in the lab – clocking up to 60–80 hours per week, while managing to keep up with her family duties.

Because Yalow was confident and ambitious, she was often called 'abrasive' or 'aggressive' but she didn't care. For years, she had to face criticism at work, including from women, but she never quit nor turned her back on other young women, especially if she believed they had the potential to become scientists. She said that as far as she was concerned "There was something wrong with the discriminators, not something wrong with me."

1959: The RIA Era Begins

It's almost poetic that Yalow was born in 1921, the same year as the discovery of insulin. In 1947, Yalow joined the Bronx Veterans Administration Hospital as a part-time consultant, and by 1950, she joined the VA full time. There she met Berson, where their first work was on using radioisotopes in blood volume determination, diagnosing thyroid diseases, and the kinetics of iodine metabolism. "It seemed obvious to apply these methods to smaller peptides, i.e., the hormones," Yalow wrote in her Nobel autobiography. "Insulin was the hormone most readily available in a highly purified form… In studying the reaction of insulin with antibodies, we appreciated that we had developed a tool with the potential for measuring circulating insulin… In 1959, Yalow and Berson perfected their measurement technique and named it radioimmunoassay (RIA). RIA is extremely sensitive. It can measure one trillionth of a gram of material per millilitre of blood.

Thus "the era of radioimmunoassay (RIA) can be said to have begun in 1959."

SOLOMON BERSON AND ROSALYN YALOW

Fig. 21. Solomon Berson, MD, and Rosalyn Yalow, PhD, teamed up to do ground breaking research within the VA Hospital for the early detection of diseases, including radioimmunoassay.

Early Life

In the 1940s, the standard assumption was that Rosalyn Sussman would be a career woman rather than a housewife. In those years, there was little possibility of combining the two. Rosalyn, however, had her own ideas. Even before her high school graduation, she had decided on both marriage and a career and never doubted her ability to achieve those two goals.

Yalow graduated from Hunter College Phi Beta Kappa, magna cum laude, with a BA in chemistry and physics, in 1941. She was the perfect candidate for a graduate fellowship, but she was turned down by one university after another. Only one admissions office was honest enough to admit the real reason: they believed that, as a Jew and a woman, she would never get a job in the field.

After she applied to Purdue University for a graduate assistantship to study physics, the university wrote back to her professor: "She is from New York. She is Jewish. She is a woman. If you can guarantee her a job afterward, we'll give her an assistantship." No guarantee was possible, and the rejection hurt, Dr. Yalow told an interviewer. "They told me that as a woman, I'd never get into graduate school in physics," she said, "so they got me a job as a secretary at the College of Physicians and Surgeons and promised that, if I were a good girl, I would take courses there."

Becoming a Physicist

At the end of the summer, just before she was scheduled to begin working, Yalow received an offer from the University of Illinois at Urbana. No clear explanation was given for this late acceptance, but it was assumed that places in the graduate program in physics were vacant as a result of the draft for World War II. Even more crucial, she was offered a teaching assistantship and would be able to support herself while studying.

At Urbana, twenty-year-old Rosalyn was the only woman among 400 faculty and teaching assistants and one of only three Jews. One of the other Jews was Aaron Yalow. She met A. Aaron Yalow, a fellow physics student who was the son of a Rabbi . Yalow, from upstate New York, was the son of an Orthodox rabbi and had entered the program at the same time as Rosalyn. The two struck up a friendship that developed into a romance. On June 6, 1943, they were married.

Both did their Ph. D. research under the guidance of the renowned nuclear physicist Maurice Goldhaber, later director of Brook haven National Laboratory. Rosalyn Yalow received her Ph. D. in 1945 with an experimental thesis on "Doubly ionized K-shell following radioactive decay." During her research work for the doctoral dissertation, Yalow spent many hours in the laboratory, where she became skilled at making and using apparatus for the measurement of radioactive substances. After returning to New York City, she worked in a research laboratory as assistant engineer – the only woman engineer – and taught physics to veterans enrolled in a pre-engineering course at Hunter College.

Since Aaron had not completed his dissertation, Yalow returned to New York to see her family before looking for work. In September 1945, Aaron joined her and worked at the same laboratory, then taught at physics at the New York State Maritime College, where he was to remain for 20 years. Rosalyn lectured in physics at her alma mater, where students who were returning veterans in a pre-engineering program considered her a "spectacular" teacher. She was restless to pursue physics research for which Hunter lacked suitable facilities, she began looking for "something useful to occupy my time," even if it meant unpaid work.

When the laboratory closed the following year, Aaron took a position as a researcher in medical physics at Montefiore Hospital and Rosalyn returned to Hunter College, where she taught physics. Although she also wanted a research position, such jobs were not routinely offered to women.

It was through her husband's encouragement and help that Yalow made contact with Bernard Roswit of the Bronx Veterans Administration

Hospital. In 1947, the Veterans Administration hospitals had launched a research program to explore the use of radioactive substances for the diagnosis and treatment of disease. One of the hospitals chosen for this nuclear medicine project was the Bronx VA Hospital. Roswit was impressed with Rosalyn Yalow's ability and determination and offered her laboratory space and a small salary as a consultant in nuclear physics. She held that position, together with her faculty position at Hunter, for three years. In 1950, she was appointed physicist and assistant chief of the hospital's radioisotope service and left her teaching post for full-time research.

Because she did not feel it was sufficiently challenging for a full-time career, she volunteered to work in the laboratory of Dr. Edith Quimby at the College of Physicians and Surgeons of Columbia University, to learn the medical applications of radioisotopes. Through Dr. Quimby, she met Dr. G. Failla, one of the foremost physicists in the country. He introduced her to Dr. Bernard Roswit, Chief of Radiotherapy at the Bronx VA Hospital, who hired her as a part-time consultant to equip and develop the Radioisotope Service. In January 1950, she resigned from the faculty of Hunter College and went to work at the Bronx VA Hospital full time.

In the spring of 1950, Dr. Yalow realized she needed an associate with a clinical background in medicine, but was unable to find someone to meet her standards. She consulted Dr. Bernard Straus, Chief of Medicine at the Bronx VA Hospital. He introduced her to Dr. Solomon Berson, whom he described "as the brightest physician I have ever trained." Although Dr. Berson had already committed himself to a position in the VA Hospital in Bedford, Massachusetts, he had a long interview with Dr. Yalow, during which they challenged each other with mathematical problems. Later, commenting on the interview, she stated, "After half an hour, I knew he was the smartest person I had ever met." He must have been equally impressed by her, because he resigned his prior commitment and joined Dr. Yalow at the Bronx VA Hospital.

Yalow and Berson Team Up

At first Yalow had only an old janitor's closet to use as a laboratory, and since her field was so new, she often had to build her own equipment. In 1950 Solomon Berson, a highly recommended medical doctor, came to work with her. For the next 22 years Yalow and Berson worked together using radioactive isotopes to study what happens inside the human body.

Berson too had grown up as a brilliant child in New York City. His Russian immigrant father applied his chemical engineering degree from Columbia University in the fur-dying industry. Young Berson became an accomplished violinist and chess player among other developed talents. After graduating from the City College of New York in 1938, he applied to several medical schools but was not accepted. Instead, he received an MS degree at New York University and began to teach anatomy in NYU's dental school. In 1941 he was admitted to NYU's medical school and subsequently served his internship at Boston City Hospital and his residency at the Bronx VA hospital, where he encountered Yalow. The first year he also moonlighted in the private practice of medicine, which he enjoyed very much. However, due to the demands of the research work in which he had become involved, he discontinued the part-time practice

Joint Research Programme (From Autobiography)

To return to the scientific aspects of my life, after Sol joined our Service, I soon gave up collaborative work with others and concentrated on our joint researches. Our first investigations together were in the application of radioisotopes in blood volume determination, clinical diagnosis of thyroid diseases and the kinetics of iodine metabolism. We extended these techniques to studies of the distribution of globins, which had been suggested for use as a plasma expander, and of serum proteins. It seemed obvious to apply these methods to smaller peptides, i.e., the hormones. Insulin was the hormone most readily available in a highly purified form. We soon deduced from the retarded rate of disappearance of insulin from the circulation of insulin-treated subjects that all these patients develop antibodies to the animal insulin. In studying the reaction of insulin with antibodies, we appreciated that we had developed a tool with the potential for measuring circulating insulin. It took several more years of work to transform the concept into the reality of its practical application to the measurement of plasma insulin in man. Thus, **the era of radioimmunoassay (RIA) can be said to have begun in 1959.** RIA is now used to measure hundreds of substances of biologic interest in thousands of laboratories in our country and abroad, even in scientifically less advanced lands.

It is of interest from this brief history that neither Sol nor I had the advantage of specialized post-doctoral training in investigation. We learned from and disciplined each other and were probably each other's severest critic. I had the good fortune to learn medicine not in a formal medical school but directly from a master of physiology, anatomy, and clinical medicine. This training was essential if I were to use my scientific background in areas in which I had no formal education.

It was generally known in their laboratory that Berson and Yalow liked to work by themselves, sometimes even to the point of washing their own glassware. They had a large joint office, to which the office door was always closed. They liked to do their own thinking and have their own discussions in private. They were both very diligent and devoted to their work, to the point that the time of the day or night was not permitted to interrupt an experiment or project on which they were working. This self-discipline was carried over to their limitation of the number of their research fellows, usually two at a time for a year or two, followed by a similar period without any, after which they would take on one or two more for a few years. The explanation given for this was that much though they enjoyed teaching, the time it detracted from their research was more than they wanted to forgo.

Yalow and Berson began a research partnership that was to last 22 years, until Berson's untimely death in 1972. Their joint investigations began with an attempt to use radioisotopes to obtain more accurate estimates of blood volume, but their first major contribution was a study of how the thyroid gland and kidneys remove iodine from the blood. They developed a method of discerning the quantity of blood cleared of iodine by the thyroid gland per unit of time. Using radioisotopes, Yalow and Berson could readily ascertain clearance rates in a 35-min sitting, providing a quick determination of thyroid activity.

Expanding these measuring techniques to the study of globins and other serum proteins, Yalow and Berson were determined to apply their methods to one of the most important classes of small peptides: hormones. According to Yalow, they chose insulin as a subject of research because it was the hormone most readily available in a purified form and was easier to work with in the laboratory than other hormones. But Yalow had a familial reason to be interested in insulin, as her husband, Aaron, was diabetic. Among the endocrine gland disorders, diabetes affects the greatest number of people, making insulin uniquely important. Without insulin and its ability to lower blood sugar, death is inevitable.

This was the first real proof that so small a protein could stimulate an immunologic response. The scientific establishment was reluctant to accept such a finding, and the two researchers had difficulty publishing their paper. The results were eventually published in 1959, and when their observations were confirmed by others, the significance of the discovery was clear. Not only had they proven that the human immune system could recognize and respond to smaller molecules than previously thought possible, but they had done so using a breakthrough technology.

Yalow and Berson called their method radioimmunoassay – the first technique to use radio isotopic techniques for the study of the primary reaction of antigen with antibody. Yalow and Berson had provided a means to observe the previously invisible world of antigen – antibody reactions that take place in solution. Before their ideas and methods, scientists were restricted in the analysis of reactions between antigens and antibodies to those that produced visible precipitation or other evidence, such as the clumping of red blood cells. The development of RIA stimulated a revolution in theoretical immunology and, in point of fact, all biology.

Together, Yalow and Berson tore through hormone research, interpreting their discovery of RIA as a starting gun. What they learned allowed researchers to tell the difference between patients with type 1 and type 2 diabetes; which children would be able to benefit from human growth hormone treatments; whether ulcers should be operated on or handled with medication; which newborns needed a medical intervention for underactive thyroid…and the list goes on. Though others were slow to catch on, within a decade, the RIA technique energized scientists, transforming endocrinology into the "it" specialty in medical research. For eighteen years, Yalow and Berson knocked out hormone after hormone, furiously preparing solutions and loading 2,000 to 3,000 test tubes in twenty-four-hour stretches.

By the time Berson moved on to City University of New York in 1968, much of RIA-related research had already been worked out. Even so, Berson and Yalow reunited on Tuesdays and Thursdays to pull all-nighters at the lab.

In a terrible one-two punch, Berson was hit with a small stroke in March, 1972 and then a heart attack during a scientific conference in Atlantic City one month later. The heart attack killed him.

Berson and Yalow were so close that their relationship was nearly familial, and his death hit Yalow extraordinarily hard. Besides losing her friend and research partner, she was concerned about losing her status. For their entire partnership, his had been their outward-facing image. Yalow was devastated by his death, but she also didn't want the public interest in her work to be buried with Berson.

Berson's death was Yalow's "low point, both professionally and personally." After his demise Yalow had to show that she was "more than just his technician." No surviving member of a scientific team had ever received a Nobel Prize. At a dedication ceremony on April 4, 1974, she named her research laboratory, where she had become chief of nuclear medicine in 1970, in honour or her collaborator of 22 years. In 1968 she became research professor at the Mount Sinai School of Medicine, where she was appointed distinguished service professor (1974–79), and where in 1986 she became the first Solomon A. Berson Distinguished Professor at large. Yalow was showered with numerous honours, including the prestigious Albert Lasker Basic Medical Research Award (the first woman to win it), which is often a precursor of the Nobel Prize in physiology or medicine, the National Medal of Science (the United States' highest science award), and more than 50 honorary degrees.

Combining Work and Family

According to policy at the VA, women had to leave once they were five months pregnant, but Yalow ignored it. During those early years of research, Rosalyn and Aaron Yalow had their first child, a son, Benjamin, born in 1952. The young mother was back in her laboratory a week later, together with her baby. She continued her lab work while she nursed the baby, managing it all on very little sleep. When she gave birth to her daughter, Elanna, in 1954, she followed the same procedure. She was conscious of the responsibilities of motherhood and tried hard not to neglect her children. While they were in school, she came home every day to give them lunch and maintained a kosher home in deference to her husband's wishes. She was home in time to prepare dinner every evening, sometimes returning to her laboratory afterward, working long into the night. She routinely maintained a work schedule of sixty to eighty hours per week. Rosalyn Yalow, proud of her accomplishments, never regretted not patenting RIA. Had she done so, she would have been a rich woman. However, she claimed to have always felt uncomfortable having "more money than I can spend usefully." As she told a *New York Post* reporter, "I have my marriage, two wonderful children. I have a laboratory that is an absolute joy. I have energy. I have health. As long as there is anything to be done, I am never tired."

Yalow's grown children are both successful professionals in their own right. Benjamin Yalow has an MBA from New York University and is a computer systems analyst; he also plays a central role in the world of science fiction fandom. Elanna Yalow has a PhD in Educational Psychology from the Stanford University Graduate School of Education and an MBA from Stanford University School of Business and is Chief Executive Officer of Kinder Care Education.

At the age of seventy-one, Yalow officially retired and became Senior Medical Investigator Emerita at the VA Hospital and the Solomon A. Berson distinguished professor-at-large at Mount Sinai School of Medicine in New York. She came to the lab several times a week and claimed to be still cooking dinners nightly for her husband, a physics professor at Cooper Union College in New York City . She continued to respond to mail, give interviews, and help students at the VA's Berson laboratory. Her husband, Dr. Aaron Yalow died in 1992, at the age of 72, from cardiac arrest.

Carving Out Time for Family

Glick (one of the Research students), recalls that Yalow worked extremely long hours, arriving at the lab early and staying late. Even with her other responsibilities, including her husband and two children, she took good care of what she called her professional family, the researchers like Glick who worked in her lab. She was protective, Glick recalls, and would intervene if anyone attacked the lab members' work in print or at conferences. "She was like a lioness with her cubs," he says.

Team Break up

Yalow and Berson's partnership broke up in 1968 when he left to run a department at the Mount Sinai hospital. He died four years later, leaving Yalow to continue probing the roles of insulin and other hormones. Researchers in her field agreed that the development of radioimmunoassay was worthy of major scientific awards. However, her peers weren't sure whether a woman would receive such distinctions when her male collaborator had died. But in 1976, Yalow became the first woman to win the Albert Lasker Basic Medical Science Award. In 1977, she shared the Nobel Prize with two male recipients who had worked on unrelated research.

Rejection of their Ideas

In the mid-1950s Yalow and Berson discovered that the blood sera of all patients who had been treated with insulin contained specific antibodies to insulin. Unfortunately, the prevailing wisdom at that time was that insulin was too small a molecule to produce an antibody, and when Yalow and Berson tried to publish their findings, their carefully constructed paper was rejected in 1955 by the US Journal of Clinical Investigation, while the cautious research journal Science asked them to refer to specific "immunoglobulin's" rather than insulin "antibodies".

Yalow and Berson knew that they were right. They saw that specific antibodies were the key to techniques which could have huge value in endocrinology and other aspects of clinical medicine. They were infuriated that their years of investigation could be so casually rejected. This episode embittered Yalow for the rest of her life, but its immediate effect was to stimulate an increase in the scope and precision of her research to produce results which, in the end, nobody could refute.

Copy of the letter of Rejection

LORRAINE 8 6716

5531

THE JOURNAL OF CLINICAL INVESTIGATION
Published and Edited by The American Society For Clinical Investigation
622 WEST 168TH STREET
NEW YORK 32, NEW YORK

September 29, 1955

Dr. Solomon A. Berson
Radioisotope Service
Veterans Administration Hospital
130 West Kingsbridge Road
Bronx 68, New York

Dear Dr. Berson:

I regret that the revision of your paper entitled "Insulin-I^{131} Metabolism in Human Subjects: Demonstration of Insulin Transporting Antibody in the Circulation of Insulin Treated Subjects" is not acceptable for publication in THE JOURNAL OF CLINICAL INVESTIGATION. — — — — — — — — — — — —

— — — — — — — — — — — — — — — The second major criticism relates to the dogmatic conclusions set forth which are not warranted by the data. The experts in this field have been particularly emphatic in rejecting your positive statement that the "conclusion that the globulin responsible for insulin binding is an acquired antibody appears to be inescapable". They believe that you have not demonstrated an antigen-antibody reaction on the basis of adequate criteria, nor that you have definitely proved that a globulin is responsible for insulin binding, nor that insulin is an antigen. The data you present are indeed suggestive but any more positive claim seems unjustifiable at present.

— —

Sincerely,

Stanley E. Bradley, M.D.
Editor-in-Chief

SEB/scn
Encl.

List of Awards of Rosalyn Sussman Yalow

1. Yalow was awarded a Fulbright fellowship to Portugal, which is an American scholarship program of competitive, merit-based grants that sponsor participants for exchanges in all areas of endeavour, including the sciences, business, academe, public service, government, and the arts.

2. In 1961, Yalow won the Eli Lilly Award of the American Diabetes Association, which provides scholarships for up to 100 scholars to attend Scientific Sessions, the world's largest scientific and medical conference focused on diabetes and its complications. Additionally, it provides the education and training for these scholars to serve as faculty for professional education programs and to clinically manage the disease.

3. A year later, she was awarded the Gairdner Foundation International Award, which recognizes the world's most creative and accomplished biomedical scientists who are advancing humanity.

4. The same year, Yalow was awarded the **American,** which recognizes excellence and distinguished contributions by individuals to internal medicine.

5. In 1972, Yalow was awarded the **Middleton Award** for Excellence in Research, which is the highest honour awarded annually by the Biomedical Laboratory Research and Development Service to senior biomedical research scientists in recognition of their outstanding scientific contributions and achievements, pertaining to the healthcare of veterans.

6. Also in 1972, she was given the Koch Award of the Endocrine Society, which awards individuals for their dedication to excellence in research, education, and clinical practice in the field of endocrinology.

7. In 1975, Yalow and Berson (who had died in 1972) were awarded the **American,** which is a gold medallion award presented to

individuals on special occasions in recognition of their outstanding work in scientific achievement.

8. The following year (1976) she became the first female recipient and first nuclear physicist of the **Albert**. Established by Albert and Mary Lasker in 1945, the award is intended to celebrate scientists who have made fundamental biological discoveries and clinical advances that improve human health.

9. In 1977, Yalow was the sixth individual woman (seventh overall, considering Marie Curie's two wins), and first American-born woman, to win the Nobel Prize in a scientific field. She was also the second woman in the world to win in the physiology or medicine category (the first was Gerty Cori). Yalow was honoured for her role in devising the radioimmunoassay technique, along with Roger Guillemin and Andrew V. Schally for their research in another field . By measuring substances in the human body, the screening of the blood of donors for such diseases as hepatitis was made possible. Radioimmunoassay can be used to measure a multitude of substances found in tiny quantities in fluids within and outside of organisms (such as viruses, drugs, and hormones). The list of substances is endless, but specifically, it allowed blood donations to be screened for various types of hepatitis. The technique can also be used to identify hormone-related health problems. Further, it can be used to detect

10. in the blood many foreign substances including some cancers. Finally, the technique can be used to measure the effectiveness of dose levels of antibiotics and drugs.

11. In 1977, Yalow received the Golden Plate Award of the American Academy of Achievement.

12. In 1978, Yalow was elected a Fellow of the American Academy of Arts and Sciences, which provides an opportunity for an early-career

professional with training in science or engineering to learn about a career in public policy and administration.

13. In 1986, Yalow was awarded the A. Cressy Morrison Award in Natural Sciences of the **New**, which is offered by Mr. Abraham Cressy Morrison to individuals with superlative papers on a scientific subject within the field of The New York Academy of Sciences and its Affiliated Societies.

14. In 1988, Yalow received the **National**, which is given to American individuals who deserve the highest honour in science and technology. The National Medal of Science was awarded by the President Ronald Reagan.

15. In 1993, Yalow was inducted into the **National**.

N. B.: She continued to conduct and direct research at her VA lab until her retirement in 1991. Yalow was a distinguished service professor at **Mount Sinai School of Medicine**.

Fig. 22. Rosalyn S. Yalow and Sol. Berson in Pittsburgh with a check they won from the University of Pittsburgh.

Fig. 23. Rosalyn Yalow, Roger Unger, Solomon Berson and Erik Jorpes at the Nobel Conference on Gastrointestinal Hormones in 1970.

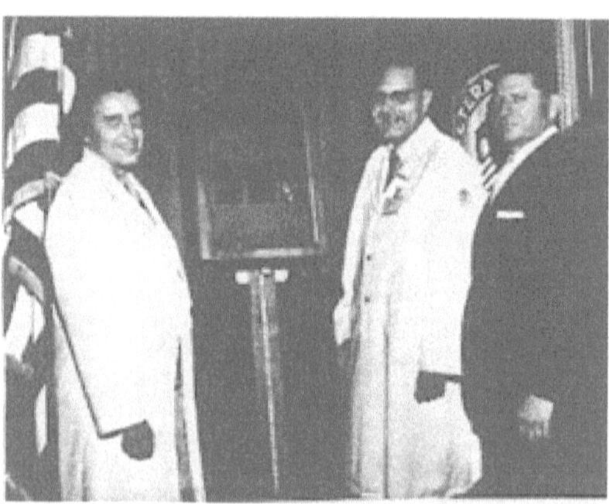

Fig. 24. Yalow (left), receiving the Middleton Award with Kenneth Sterling, MD (centre), and Bronx VA Medical Centre Director Harold Jaffrey (right)

Fig. 25. Rosalyn Yalow at a Veterans Administration Center meeting in California in December of 1978.

Education of Rosalyn Sussmanyalow

B. A. Physics, Hunter College, 1941

M. S. Physics, University of Illinois, 1942

Ph. D. Physics, University of Illinois, 1945

Diploma, American Board of Radiology, 1951

Jobs/Positions

1941–43 Assistant in Physics, University of Illinois

1944–45 Instructor in Physics, University of Illinois

1945–46 Assistant Engineer, Federal Telecommunications Laboratory

1946–50 Lecturer and Assistant Professor of Physics, Hunter College

1947–50 Consultant, Radioisotope Unit, Veterans Administration Hospital, Bronx, NY

1950–70 Physicist and Assistant Chief, Radioisotope Unit, Veterans Administration Hospital, Bronx, NY

1963–91 Research Professor, Mt. Sinai School of Medicine

1968–70 Acting Chief, Radioisotope Unit, Veterans Administration Hospital, Bronx, NY

1968–74 Research Professor, Mt. Sinai School of Medicine

1970–86 Chief, Nuclear Medicine Service, Veterans Administration Hospital, Bronx, NY

1972–91 Senior Medical Investigator, Veterans Administration Hospital, Bronx, NY

1973–79 Co-Editor, *Hormone and Metabolic Research*

1974–79 Distinguished Service Professor, Mt. Sinai School of Medicine

1979–85 Distinguished Professor at Large, Albert Einstein College of Medicine, Yeshiva University

1980–85 Chair, Department of Clinical Science, Montefiore Hospital and Medical Center

1986-present Emeritus Professor, Albert Einstein College of Medicine, Yeshiva University

Honors

Nobel Prize in Medicine 1977

for the development of radioimmunoassay of peptide hormones

National Medal of Science, 1988

Member, American Academy of Arts and Science

Member, National Academy of Sciences

Fellow, New York Academy of Science

Member, American College of Nuclear Physician

Associate Fellow in Physics, American College of Radiology

Partial Listing of Awards

Eli Lilly Award, American Diabetes Association, 1961

Federal Woman's Award,1961 (*Not accepted; she refused awards restricted to women because, in her view, they represent reverse discrimination and their existence implies women are not competitive in the broader scientific field.*

Van Slyke Award, American Association of Clinical Chemists, 1968

Gairdner Foundation International Award,1971

American College of Physicians Award, 1971

Koch Award, Endocrine Society, 1972

A. Cressy Morrison Award in Natural Sciences, New York Academy of Sciences, 1975

Scientific Achievement Award, American Medical Association, 1975

Boehringer-Mannheim Award, American Association of Clinical Chemists, 1975

Modern Medicine's Distinguished Achievement Award, 1976

Albert Lasker Basic Medical Research Award,1976

American Academy of Achievement Golden Plate Award for Salute to Excellence, 1977

La Madonnina International Prize of Milan, 1977

Alumni Association Achievement Award, University of Illinois, 1978

Banting Medal, American Diabetes Association, 1978

Gratum Genus Humanum Gold Medal, World Federation of Nuclear Medicine and Biology, 1978

Rosalyn S. Yalow Research and Development Award, 1978

Theobold Smith Award, 1982

George Charles de Henesy Nuclear Medicine Pioneer Award, 1986

Inducted into the National Women's Hall of Fame, 1993

Honorary Doctorates

Honorary Doctorates from many UNIVERSITIES including Bar-Ilan University (Israel),

Columbia University,

Hunter College,

Johns Hopkins University,

New York Medical College,

Princeton University,

University of Ghent (Belgium),

Universite Claude Bernard, (France),

University of Illinois (Champaign, IL, United States),

Washington University (Seattle, Washington, United States), and

Yeshiva University (500 W 185th St, New York, NY 10033, United States).

Important Dates in the Life of Rosalyn Yalow

July 19, 1921 Birth. New York (N. Y.).

1941 B. A. degree in Chemistry and Physics, Hunger College, New York (N. Y.).

1945 Ph. D. in Nuclear Physics, University of Illinois, Urbana-Champaign, Urbana (Ill.).

1945 Assistant Engineer, Federal Telecommunications Laboratory, ITT, New York (N. Y.).

1946–1950 Physics Instructor, Hunter College, New York (N. Y.).

1947–2011 Consultant; Researcher; Acting Chief of the Radioisotope Service (1968); Chief of the Nuclear Medicine Service (1970); Senior Medical Investigator emeritus (1972–2011); and Director of the Solomon A. Berson Research Laboratory (1973), Bronx Veterans Administration Hospital, Bronx (New York, N. Y.).

1950–1972 Partnered with Solomon A. Berson on radioisotope research.

1959 Yalow and Berson present their discovery of radioimmunoassay (RIA).

1961 Awarded the Eli Lilly Award, American Diabetes Association.

1968–1986 Research Professor; Distinguished Service Professor (1974) ; Solomon A. Berson Distinguished professor at large (1986), Mount Sinai School of Medicine, New York (N. Y.).

1976 Awarded the Albert Lasker Prize for Basic Medical Research, Lasker Foundation.

1977 Awarded the Nobel Prize in Physiology or Medicine in 1977 alongside Andrew B Schally and Roger Guillemin "for the development of radioimmunoassay of peptide hormones".

1978 Member, American Academy of Arts and Sciences.

1980 Distinguished Professor at large, Albert Einstein College of Medicine, Yeshiva University.

1981 Acting Chairperson, Department of Clinical Sciences, Montefiore Medical Center.

May 30, 2011 Death. New York (N. Y.).

Death

Yalow died May 30, 2011, in the Bronx, New York. She was predeceased by her husband, and survived by two children, Benjamin, and Elanna, and two grandchildren. She was buried at Mount Moriah Cemetery in Fairview, New Jersey.

Occupation

Medical Physicist

Places

Birth

New York (N. Y.)

Undergraduate Education

New York (N. Y.)

Graduate Education

Urbana (Ill.)

Employment

Bronx (New York, N. Y.)

New York (N. Y.)

Death

New York (N. Y.)

Subjects

Medical physics.

Physiology.

Radioisotopes.

Women in science.

Relationships

PEOPLE

Family

Yalow, Elanna S.

Daughter.

Advisors & Collaborators

Berson, Solomon A., 1918–1972

Partnered together for 22 years to discover and develop radioimmunoassay.

Dresselhaus, M. S.

Advised by Yalow, Hunter College.

Goldhaber, Maurice, 1911–2011

PhD advisor at University of Illinois, Urbana-Champaign in Immunochemistry.

Schoenheimer, Rudolf, 1898–1941

Advisor, Columbia University.

Straus, Eugene

Collaborated at Solomon A. Berson Research Laboratory.

Additional

Curie, Marie, 1867–1934

Failla, Gioacchino

Fermi, Enrico, 1901–1954

Quimby, Edith H. (Edith Hinkley), 1891–1982

Institutions
Major Positions

Hunter College

B. A in Chemistry and Physics (1941); and Physics Lecturer.

ITT Corporation

Assistant engineer.

Montefiore Medical Center

Acting Chairperson, Department of Clinical Sciences.

Mount Sinai School of Medicine

Research Professor; Distinguished Service Professor; and Solomon A. Berson Distinguished Professor at large.

Veterans Administration Hospital (Bronx, New York, N. Y.)

Consultant; Researcher; Acting Chief of the Radioisotope service (1968); Chief of the Nuclear Medicine Service; Senior Medical Investigator emeritus (1972–2011); and Director of the Solomon A. Berson Research Laboratory (1973).

Yeshiva University

Distinguished Professor at large, Albert Einstein College of Medicine.

Professional Activities & Affiliations

Albert and Mary Lasker Foundation

Awarded the Albert Lasker Prize for Basic Medical Research (1976).

American Academy of Arts and Sciences

Fellow

American Diabetes Association

Awarded the Eli Lilly Award (1961).

University of Illinois at Urbana-Champaign

PhD in Nuclear Physics (1945).

Resources

Archival Resources

Author

AAPM interviews with physicists in medicine [video recordings], 1990–2014.

Niels Bohr Library & Archives

American Institute of Physics

One Physics Ellipse, College Park, MD 20740, USA

Rosalyn Yalow papers.

Clark T. Awin Memorial Library.

Endocrine Society

8401 Connecticut Avenue, Suite 900 Chevy Chase, MD 20815–5817, USA

Published Resources

Subject

Academic Tree: Rosalyn Yalow professional relations list.

American Nuclear Society Nuclear Café: Women's History Month – Physicist Dr. Rosalyn Sussman Yalow.

Contributions of 20th century women to physics [online resource], 1900–1976.

Jewish Women's Archive: Rosalyn Yalow biography.

New York Time's Yalow obituary.

Nobel Prize Laureate Rosalyn Yalow biography and facts.

Physics Today obituary: Rosalyn Yalow.

Rosalyn Yalow, Nobel laureate: her life and work in medicine: a biographical memoir / by Eugene Straus.

19 Jul 1921

Bronx, Bronx County, New York, USA

Death

30 May 2011 (aged 89)

Bronx, Bronx County, New York, USA

Burial

Mount Moriah Cemetery

Fairview, Bergen County, New Jersey, USA.

Dr. Aaron Yalow (A Brief Note)

Dr. Aaron Yalow, a retired professor of physics at the Cooper Union School of Engineering and a medical physicist at the Hospital for Joint Diseases, died on Saturday at Montefiore Medical Center. He was 72 years old and lived in the Bronx.

His family said he died of cardiac arrest.

Dr. Yalow retired from Cooper Union and the hospital in 1982.

His wife of 49 years, Dr. Rosalyn Sussman Yalow, shared the Nobel Prize in Medicine in 1977 with Dr. Roger C. L. Guillemin and Dr. Andrew V. Schally.

Dr. Yalow is survived by his wife; a son, Benjamin, of the Bronx; a daughter, Elanna Yalow of Larkspur, Calif.; a sister, Chaniett Lerner of Brooklyn, and two grandchildren.

**A version of this article appears in print on Aug. 11, 1992, Section D, Page19 of the National edition with the headline: Dr. Aaron Yalow; Professor, 72.

Solomon A. Berson (1918–1972)

By: *Jennifer R. Craer*
Published: *2013-11-01*

Solomon A. Berson helped develop the radioimmunoassay (RIA) technique in the US during the twentieth century. Berson made many scientific contributions while working with research partner Rosalyn Yalow at the Bronx Veterans Administration (VA) hospital, in New York City, New York. In the more than twenty years that Berson and Yalow collaborated, they refined the procedures for tracing diagnostic biological compounds using isotope labels. In the late 1950s they developed the RIA based on the ability to trace the competition between and ligands, or small molecules that bind to specific sites of other bio molecules, and proteins for the same molecular binding site, a process called competitive binding. Scientists widely used Berson and Yalow's RIA, as these methods permit the use of a minimal sample of blood for accurate measurements of biological molecules such as hormones that cause the production of antibodies. Berson and Yalow's research has advanced the study of physiology, including that of the reproductive system, with particular applications to the diagnosis and treatment of infertility.

Berson was born on 22 April, 1918, in New York City, and was the eldest of three children. His father, an immigrant from Russia, studied chemical engineering before becoming a business owner. Throughout his early schooling, Berson played music and chess. In 1938 Berson completed his undergraduate studies at (**NYU**), in New York City, and he tried to pursue a medical career. However, every medical school to which he applied rejected him, so he returned to NYU to complete a master's degree in science, which he received in 1939. Berson then accepted a teaching fellowship at the NYU College of Dentistry, which he held until he was able to start attending the NYU School of Medicine in 1941. While pursuing his MD, Berson married Miriam Gittleson in 1942, with whom he would later have two daughters, Wendy and Debby.

Berson completed his medical degree in 1945 and spent the following year interning at Boston City Hospital, in Boston, Massachusetts, before serving in the military for two years. After his time in the US Army, Berson completed a two-year residency in internal medicine at the Bronx VA Hospital. He planned to join the staff at the VA hospital in Bedford, Massachusetts, but he also considered staying at the Bronx VA to work with Yalow, Assistant Chief of the Radioisotope Service in the Radiotherapy Department.

Fig. 26. Solomon Berson (1918–1972)

Solomon Berson

Date of Birth	April 22, 1918
Place of Birth	New York, USA
Date of death	April 11, 1972
Place of death	Atlantic City, US

Yalow was seeking a physician of internal medicine to provide background knowledge for her research. After an interview during which the two discussed various mathematical puzzles, Berson agreed to remain in New York to conduct research with Yalow. Berson and Yalow's diverse backgrounds, in internal medicine and nuclear physics, respectively, produced a partnership focused on nuclear medicine, more specifically on the development of medical applications of radioisotopes. The duo first focused on using radioiodine (isotope iodine I-131) to study the rates of iodine production and degradation in humans—studies that contributed to the understanding of thyroid metabolism and disorders. Berson and Yalow further developed their radioactive labelling method to test whether abnormally rapid degradation of insulin by the enzyme insulinase caused adult diabetes, a hypothesis their findings did not support.

Berson, Yalow, and colleagues studied the metabolism of insulin in diabetic and non-diabetic subjects by monitoring how quickly insulin was cleared from the blood by the kidneys, referred to as the clearance rate. Clearance rates were tracked by using livestock – derived insulin that had been bound to radioactive iodine, creating radioiodine-labelled insulin. Berson and Yalow injected the insulin into human subjects and collected sequential blood samples to track clearance rates. They discovered that people previously treated with insulin could not clear insulin from their blood as quickly as untreated subjects. The research team postulated that human subjects that had previously been treated with insulin had a slower clearance rate because the bodies of these subjects recognized the livestock-derived insulin as a foreign substance. Recognition of foreign molecules would then trigger specific immune system globulins to bind to and degrade the insulin. The binding of globulins causes the body to retain the insulin over a longer period, rather than quickly clearing the unbound insulin from the blood through the urine. Berson, Yalow, and colleagues submitted their findings to **Science and *The Journal of Clinical Investigation*** (JCI), but both journals rejected their submission, as reviewers did not support the idea that insulin could cause the body to produce antibodies. After much argument, the research team replaced the controversial term insulin antibody with the phrase insulin globulin binding and the paper was published in JCI in 1956.

In 1960, Berson and Yalow published "Immunoassay of Endogenous Plasma Insulin in Man," in which they described the details of the radioactive labelling method for the scientific community. They were aware of the commercial potential of RIA, yet they refused to patent the method, and they encouraged other researchers to expand RIA applications. By 2012, the 1960 article had greater than 2,500 citations.

Throughout the 1960s Berson served on the US National Advisory Council. He received several honours, including the Eli Lilly Award of the American Diabetes Association in 1957 and the William S. Middleton Research Award in 1960. In 1968 Berson became professor and chairman of the Department of Medicine at the Mount Sinai School of Medicine, within the City University of New York, in New York City. Yalow claimed that Berson's acceptance of that position was a great loss for the scientific community because he did less research than he had before. In April of 1972 Berson was elected to the USNational Academy of Sciences. That same month, he died from a heart attack while attending a conference for the Federation of American Societies for Experimental Biology in Atlantic City, New Jersey.

In remembrance of Berson's contributions, Yalow requested that the Radioisotope Service laboratory be renamed the Solomon A. Berson

Research Laboratory. In 1977 Yalow received the Nobel Prize in Physiology or Medicine for the co-discovery of RIA. Though Yalow honoured Berson for his involvement in that discovery, the Nobel Committee does not award posthumous prizes.

Life of Solomon Berson in the Hospital and Communities

In addition to doing research, Dr. Berson was a superbly lucid and vigorous lecturer and teacher. His quick, sharp questions and comments enlivened all meetings he attended or chaired. He was also one of the busiest referees of scientific manuscripts. Editors of several prominent journals called on him especially to referee works that contained complicated mathematics. Since Dr. Berson was a self-taught expert in both mathematics and physics, especially as applied to biological research, he was not discouraged by the mathematical complexities of some contemporary works.

Comments of co-workers in the Laboratory of Yalow

An admirable characteristic of Berson and Yalow is that they always welcomed visiting scientists to their laboratory and were never reluctant to teach them their methods or to help them use the RIA technique to identity additional proteins for their own particular research use.

With all respect to their disciples, I think recognition of the achievements of Berson and Yalow by the scientific community is worthy of reiteration. Berson was a member of the National Academy of Sciences and Professor of Medicine and Chairman of the Department of Medicine at Mount Sinai School of Medicine. **Dr. Bernard Straus once said of Dr. Berson, "He is the brightest physician I have ever trained."** In interviewing Dr. Shimon Glick, another co-worker of the Berson and Yalow laboratory, he said, "When we first began to work with Berson and Yalow, we quickly developed an inferiority complex because Berson was so smart it was beyond comprehension. **He was a real renaissance man; higher mathematics for him was like ABC. He was violinist, a connoisseur of the arts, and a phenomenal chess player. I mean, he was just an unbelievable guy."** In Dr. Yalow's biographical summary at The Nobel Prize Awards Ceremony, she said, "Sol's leaving the laboratory in 1968 to assume the Chairmanship of the Department of Medicine at Mount Sinai School of Medicine and his premature death four years later were a great loss to investigative medicine. At my request, the laboratory which we shared has been designated The Solomon A. Berson Research Laboratory so his name will continue to be on my papers as long as I publish and so that his contributions to our Service will be memorialized."

Popularity of Dr. Solomon Berson amongst the Scholars

As a teacher of research fellows, he was most zealous and energetic. Because the Veterans Hospital could not supply the formal classes of a vast graduate centre, he himself often provided his fellows with formal didactic courses in mathematics, biochemistry, and physics. In addition to being an excellent scientist and teacher, he was a superb physician: He had a large group of loyal and devoted patients who were given warm and attentive care at regular intervals. After moving to the Mt. Sinai School of Medicine, medical students and, even more prominently, interns and residents became his principal students, and the bond between him and his house officers was very strong. His skill extended well beyond medicine and science, however; he was an accomplished violinist and chess player and was well read in history, philosophy, and art.

Popularity of Dr. Berson in the Hospital

Dr. Berson continued his research at the Radioisotope Service until his death, but in 1968 accepted the professorship and chairmanship of the Department of Medicine, at the Mount Sinai School of Medicine of the City University of New York. In this position, he influenced many medical students and house staff. When he had an argument with the administration at Mount Sinai and threatened to resign, the entire house staff on the medical service agreed to resign en masse if he were to leave. Needless to say, the dispute was adjudicated and both Dr. Berson and the house staff stayed on. In spite of the heavy demands of being professor of medicine and chairman of the department in a large medical school, Dr. Berson retained close ties with Dr. Yalow and their laboratory, and the productivity of their scientific collaboration continued unabated.

Death

On April 11, 1972, the world lost one of its outstanding citizens—Dr. Solomon A. Berson. shortly before his fifty-fourth birthday. Berson died of a heart attack in Atlantic while attending a FASEB meeting . Upon his death he was survived by his widow and two daughters.

The Solomon A. Berson Medical Alumni Achievement Award was created in Berson's honour by NYU School of Medicine.

Tragedy of Berson's Death

The tragedy of Dr. Berson's death was compounded several weeks later by the sudden death of his elder daughter, Wendy, at the age of twenty-four. He is survived by his wife, daughter, sister, and brother, and is mourned by co-workers, colleagues, students, and friends all over the world.

Scientific Career of Solomon Berson

Berson's scientific work started in 1950, when he became a member of the Radioisotope Service of the hospital, where he teamed with Rosalyn Yalow in what eventually became an historic research partnership. He also set up a thyroid service, where his approach was felt lastingly. Their early laboratory work concerned iodine and human serum albumin metabolism, but later on in the decade they shifted their focus to insulin, a hormone which was difficult to measure in the blood . They developed the radioimmunoassay, which gave very good results, and published their findings in 1960. They were able to distinguish between two types of diabetes, Type I and Type II , which have significantly different mechanisms.

With the success of the insulin RIA , Berson and Yalow extended their success to other hormones, such as corticotropin, gastrin, parathyroid hormone and growth hormone, making significant discoveries in their physiology along the way.

Awards received by Solomon Berson

1. Berson, usually together with Yalow, received numerous awards for his work. In 1968, he was elected Murray M. Rosenberg Professor and Chair of Medicine at **Medicine of** the City University of New York , enjoying great popularity.

2. He also served on the editorial boards of several medical journals.

3. He was elected to the National Academy of Sciences in 1972.

4. In 1975, Berson and Yalow received the AMA Scientific Achievement Award (Berson posthumously), and two years later Yalow received a Nobel Prize (which cannot be awarded posthumously) for their joint work on the radioimmunoassay.

Paper Published with Rosalyn Yalow

Solomon A. Berson 63 Selected Bibliographies

1951
With R. S. Yalow. The use of K42-tagged erythrocytes in blood volume determinations. Science, 114: 14–15.

1952

With R. S. Yalow. The effect of cortisone on the iodine accumulating function of the thyroid gland in euthyroid subjects. J. Clin. Endocrinol. Metab., 12: 407–22.

With R. S. Yalow, J. Sorrentino, and B. Roswit. The determination of thyroidal and renal plasma I1S1 clearance rates as a routine diagnostic test of thyroid dysfunction. J. Clin. Invest., 31: 141— 58.

With R. S. Yalow. The use of K42 or P32 labelled erythrocytes and I 131 tagged human serum albumins in simultaneous blood volume determinations. J. Clin. Invest., 31: 572–80.

With R. S. Yalow, A. Azulay, S. Schreiber, and B. Roswit. The biological decay curve of P32-tagged erythrocytes. Application to the study of acute changes in blood volume. J. Clin. Invest., 31: 581–91.

1953

With R. S. Yalow, J. Post, L. H. Wisham, K. N. Newerly, M. J. Villazon, and O. N. Vazquez. Distribution and fate of intravenously administered modified human globin and its effect on blood volume. Studies utilizing I131-tagged globin. J. Clin. Invest., 32: 22–32.

With R. S. Yalow, S. S. Schreiber, and J. Post. Tracer experiments with I131-labeled human serum albumin: Distribution and degradation studies. J. Clin. Invest., 32: 746–68.

1954

With R. S. Yalow. The distribution of I131-labeled human serum albumin introduced into ascitic fluid: Analysis of the kinetics of a three-compartment catenary transfer system in man and speculations on possible sites of degradation. J. Clin. Invest., 33: 377–87.

With S. S. Schreiber, A. Bauman, and R. S. Yalow. Blood volume 64 BIOGRAPHICAL MEMOIRS alterations in congestive heart failure. J. Clin. Invest., 33: 578 – 86.

With R. S. Yalow. Quantitative aspects of iodine metabolism. The exchangeable organic iodine pool, and the rates of thyroidal secretion, peripheral degradation, and faecal excretion of endogenously synthesized organically bound iodine. J. Clin. Invest., 33: 1533–52.

1955

With R. S. Yalow. Critique of extracellular space measurements with small ions: Na24 and Br82 spaces. Science, 121: 34–36.

With R. S. Yalow. The iodide trapping and binding functions of the thyroid. J. Clin. Invest., 34: 186–204.

With M. A. Rothschild, A. Bauman, and R. S. Yalow. Tissue distribution of I131-labeled human serum albumin following intravenous administration. J. Clin. Invest., 34: 1354–58.

With A. Bauman, M. A. Rothschild, and R. S. Yalow. Distribution and metabolism of I131-labeled human serum albumin in congestive heart failure with and without proteinuria. J. Clin. Invest., 34: 1359–68.

1956

With R. S. Yalow, A. Bauman, M. A. Rothschild, and K. Newerly. Insulin-I131 metabolism in human subjects: demonstration of insulin binding globulin in the circulation of insulin-treated subjects. J. Clin. Invest., 35: 170–90.

1957

With R. S. Yalow. Chemical and biological alterations induced by irradiation of I131-labeled human serum albumin. J. Clin. Invest., 36: 44–50.

With M. A. Rothschild, A. Bauman, and R. S. Yalow. The effect of large doses of desiccated thyroid on the distribution and metabolism of albumin-I1M in euthyroid subjects. J. Clin. Invest., 36: 422–28.

With R. S. Yalow. Serum protein turnover in multiple myeloma. J. Lab. Clin. Med., 49: 386–94.

With R. S. Yalow. Ethanol fractionation of plasma and electrophoretic identification of insulin-binding antibody. J. Clin. Invest., 36: 642–47.

With R. S. Yalow. Apparent inhibition of liver insulinase activity by serum and serum fractions containing insulin-binding antibody. J. Clin. Invest., 36: 648–55.

With R. S. Yalow, S. Weisenfeld, M. G. Goldner, and B. W. Volk. The effect of sulfonylureas on the rates of metabolic degradation of insulin-I131 and glucagon-I131 in vivo and in vitro. Diabetes, 6: 54–60.

With A. Bauman, M. A. Rothschild, and R. S. Yalow. Pulmonary circulation and transcapillary exchange of electrolytes. J. Appl. Physiol., 11: 353–61. With R. S. Yalow. Studies with insulin-binding antibody. Diabetes, 6: 402–7.

1958

With R. S. Yalow. Insulin antagonists, insulin antibodies and insulin resistance. Am. J. Med., 25: 155–59.

With A. B. Gutman, T. F. Yu, H. Black, and R. S. Yalow. Incorporation of glycine-1-C14, glycine-1-C14 and glycine-N15 into uric acid in normal and gouty subjects. Am. J. Med., 25: 917–32.

1959

With S. Weisenfeld and M. Pascullo. Utilization of glucose in normal and diabetic rabbits. Effects of insulin, glucagon, and glucose. Diabetes, 8: 116–27.

With R. S. Yalow. Quantitative aspects of reaction between insulin and insulin-binding antibody. J. Clin. Invest., 38: 1996–2016.

With R. S. Yalow. Species-specificity of human anti-beef, pork insulin serum. J. Clin. Invest., 38: 2017–25.

With R. S. Yalow. Assay of plasma insulin in human subjects by immunological methods. Nature, 184: 1648–49.

With R. S. Yalow. Recent studies on insulin-binding antibodies. Ann. N. Y. Acad. Sci., 82: 338–44.

1960

With R. S. Yalow. Immunoassay of endogenous plasma insulin in man. J. Clin. Invest., 39: 1157–75.

With R. S. Yalow. Plasma insulin in man (Editorial). Am. J. Med., 29: 1–8.

With R. S. Yalow. Plasma insulin concentrations in nondiabetic and early diabetic subjects. Diabetes, 9: 254–60.

With R. S. Yalow, H. Black, and M. Villazon. Comparison of plasma insulin levels following administration of tolbutamide and glucose. Diabetes, 9: 356–62.

1961

With R. S. Yalow. The effects of x-radiation of I131-labeled iodotyrosines in solution: the significance of reducing and oxidizing radicals. Radiat. Res., 14: 590–604.

With R. S. Yalow. Immunologic specificity of human insulin: application to immunoassay of insulin. J. Clin. Invest., 40: 2190–98.

With R. S. Yalow. Immunoassay of plasma insulin in man. Diabetes, 10: 339–44.

With R. S. Yalow. Preparation and purification of human insulin I 131 binding to human insulin-binding antibodies. J. Clin. Invest., 40: 1803–8.

With R. S. Yalow. Immunochemical distinction between insulins with identical amino acid sequences from different mammalian species (pork and sperm whale insulins). Nature, 191: 1392–93.

With R. S. Yalow. Plasma insulin in health and disease. Am. J. Med., 31: 874–81.

1962

With R. S. Yalow. Diverse applications of isotopically labelled insulin. Trans. N. Y. Acad. Sci., 24: 487–95.

With R. S. Yalow. Insulin antibodies and insulin resistance. Diabetes Dig., 1: 4.

1963

With R. S. Yalow. Iodine metabolism and the thyroid gland. N. Y. State J. Med., 62: 35–42.

With R. S. Yalow. Antigens in insulin: Determinants of specificity of porcine insulin in man. Science, 139: 844–85.

With R. S. Yalow, G. D. Aubarch, and J. T. Potts, Jr. Immunoassay of bovine and human parathyroid hormone. Proc. Natl. Acad. Sci. USA, 49: 613: 17.

With J. Roth, S. M. Glick, and R. S. Yalow. Hypoglycemia: A potent stimulus to secretion of growth hormone. Science, 140: 987–88.

With J. Roth, S. M. Glick, and R. S. Yalow. Secretion of human growth hormone: Physiologic and experimental modification. Metabolism, 12: 577–79.

With S. M. Glick, J. Roth, and R. S. Yalow. Immunoassay of human growth hormone in plasma. Nature, 199: 784–87.

1964

With J. Roth, S. M. Glick, and R. S. Yalow. Antibodies to human growth hormone (HGH) in human subjects treated with HGH. J. Clin. Invest., 43: 1056–65.

With R. S. Yalow. The present status of insulin antagonists in plasma. Diabetes, 13: 247–59.

With R. S. Yalow, S. M. Glick, and J. Roth. Immunoassay of protein and peptide hormones. Metabolism, 13: 1135–53.

With R. S. Yalow. Reaction of fish insulins with human insulin antiserums: Potential value in the treatment of insulin resistance. N. Engl. J. Med., 270: 1171–78.

With J. Roth, S. M. Glick, and R. S. Yalow. The influence of blood glucose and other factors on the plasma concentration of growth hormone. Diabetes, 13: 355–61.

With R. S. Yalow, S. M. Glick, and J. Roth. Radioimmunoassay of human plasma ACTH. J. Clin. Endocrinol. Metab., 24: 1219— 25.

1965

With S. M. Glick, J. Roth, and R. S. Yalow. The regulation of growth hormone secretion. In: Recent Progress in Hormone Research, ed. G. Pincus, New York: Academic Press, vol. 21, pp. 241–83.

With R. S. Yalow. Dynamics of insulin secretion in hypoglycemia. Diabetes, 14: 341–49.

With R. S. Yalow, S. M. Glick, and J. Roth. Plasma insulin and growth hormone levels in obesity and diabetes. (Conference on Adipose Tissue Metabolism and Obesity.) Ann. N. Y. Acad. Sci., 131: 357–73.

With R. S. Yalow. Some current controversies in diabetes research. Diabetes, 14: 549–72.

1966

With R. S. Yalow. Insulin in blood and insulin antibodies. Am. J. Med., 40: 676–90.

With R. S. Yalow. Iodoinsulin used to determine specific activity of Iodine-131. Science, 152: 205–7.

With R. S. Yalow. Labelling of proteins—problems and practices. Trans. N. Y. Acad. Sci., 28: 1033–44.

With R. S. Yalow. Deamidation of insulin during storage in frozen state. Diabetes, 15: 875–79.

With G. Roselin, R. Assan, and R. S. Yalow. Separation of antibody bound and unbound peptide hormones labelled with iodine131 by talcum powder and precipitated silica. Nature, 212: 355 – 57.

With R. S. Yalow. Purification of I13'-parathyroid hormone with microfine granules of precipitated silica. Nature, 212: 357–58.

With R. S. Yalow. Parathyroid hormone in plasma in adenomatous hyperparathyroidism, uremia, and bronchogenic carcinoma. Science, 154: 907–9.

With R. S. Yalow. State of human growth hormone in plasma and changes in stored solutions of pituitary growth hormone. J. Biol. Chem., 241: 5745–49.

1967

With R. S. Melick, J. R. Gill, Jr., R. S. Yalow, F. C. Bartter, J. T. Potts, Jr., and G. D. Aurbach. Antibodies and clinical resistance to parathyroid hormone. N. Engl. J. Med., 276: 144–47.

With R. S. Yalow. Radioimmunoassays of peptide hormones in plasma. N. Engl. J. Med., 277: 640–47.

1968

With R. S. Yalow. Peptide hormones in plasma. In: The Harvey Lectures, New York: Academic Press, ser. 62, 1966–1967, pp. 107 – 63.

With R. S. Yalow. Immunochemical heterogeneity of parathyroid hormone. J. Clin. Endocrinol., 28: 1037–47.

With R. S. Yalow. Radioimmunoassay of ACTH in plasma. J. Clin. Invest., 47: 2725–51.

1969

With R. S. Yalow, N. Varsano-Aharon, and E. Echemendia. HGH and ACTH secretory responses to stress. Horm. Metab. Res., 1: 3–8.

With R. S. Yalow and S. J. Goldsmith. Influence of physiologic fluctuations in plasma growth hormone on glucose tolerance. Diabetes, 18: 402–8.

With R. S. Yalow. Significance of human plasma insulin sephadex fractions. Diabetes, 18: 834–39.

1970

With R. S. Yalow. Radioimmunoassay of gastrin. Gastroenterology, 58: 1–14.

With N. Varsano-Aharon, E. Echemendia, and R. S. Yalow. Early insulin responses to glucose and to tolbutamide in maturity onset diabetes. Metabolism, 19: 409–17.

With R. S. Yalow. Size and charge distinctions between endogenous human plasma gastrin in peripheral blood and heptadecapeptide gastrins. Gastroenterology, 58: 609–15.

With S. J. Goldsmith and R. S. Yalow. Effects of 2-deoxy-d-glucose on insulin-secretory responses to intravenous glucose, glucagon, tolbutamide and arginine in man. Diabetes, 19: 453–57.

With J. H. Walsh and R. S. Yalow. Detection of Australia antigen and antibody by means of radioimmunoassay techniques. J. Infect. Dis., 121: 550–54.

1971

With J. H. Walsh and R. S. Yalow. The effect of atropine on plasma gastrin response to feeding. Gastroenterology, 60: 16–21.

With R. S. Yalow. Further studies on the nature of immunoreactive gastrin in human plasma. Gastroenterology, 60: 203–14.

With R. S. Yalow. Nature of immunoreactive gastrin extracted from tissues of gastrointestinal tract. Gastroenterology, 60: 215–22.

With G. M. A. Palmieri and R. S. Yalow. Adsorbent techniques for the separation of antibody-bound from free hormone in radioimmunoassay. Horm. Metab. Res., 3: 301–5.

With R. S. Yalow, T. Saito, and I. J. Selikoff. Antibodies to "Alcalase" after industrial exposure. N. Engl. J. Med., 284: 688–90.

With R. S. Yalow. Gastrin in duodenal ulcer. N. Engl. J. Med., 284: 445.

With R. S. Yalow. Size heterogeneity of immunoreactive human ACTH in plasma and in extracts of pituitary glands and ACTH producing thymoma. Biochem. Biophys. Res. Commun., 44: 439–45.

1972

With R. S. Yalow. Radioimmunoassay in gastroenterology. Gastroenterology, 62: 1061–84.

With G. Nilsson, J. Simon, and R. S. Yalow. Plasma gastrin and gastric acid responses to sham feeding and feeding in dogs. Gastroenterology, 63: 51–59.

With R. S. Yalow. And now, "big, big" gastrin. Biochem. Biophys. Res. Commun. 48: 391–95.

1973

With R. S. Yalow. "Big, big insulin." Metabolism, 22: 703–13.

With R. S. Yalow. Characteristics of "Big ACTH" in human plasma and pituitary extracts. J. Clin. Endocrinol. Metab., 36: 415–23

Patenting the RIA Technique

The commercial possibilities for RIA were enormous, but while Yalow and Berson recognized this, they refused to patent the method. Instead, they made every effort to get RIA into common use, putting its value to humanity ahead of their own financial interests. Yalow asserted, "We never thought of patenting RIA.... patents are about keeping things away from people for the purpose of making money. We wanted others to be able to use RIA." The seemingly inextricable connection between money and medicine was never a primary concern to Yalow. Indeed, Yalow and Berson performed all their work without ever receiving a research grant! This stands in sharp contrast to much contemporary medical research, which is corporate-sponsored and profit-oriented in the quest for intellectual property.

Dynamic Duo

After receiving her PhD in physics in 1945, Yalow returned to New York with her family, and secured a teaching position at her *alma mater*. During this time, she was intrigued by the research of George de Hevesy, a Hungarian chemist who won the Nobel Prize in 1943 for his research on the use of tracer radioisotopes in the study of chemical processes. To pursue this interest, she joined the nascent Radioisotope Service at the Bronx VA (Veterans Administration) Medical Centre in 1947. In 1950, she left her teaching duties to work full-time at the VA hospital. Solomon A Berson, a senior internal medicine resident, joined her. In their laboratory, converted from a cramped janitor's closet, Yalow and Berson would begin the research that led to their discovery of the radioimmunoassay technique. They worked together for the next 22 years, alternating first authorship on the papers they published. After Berson's passing in 1972, Yalow requested that their VA laboratory be renamed the Solomon A Berson Research Laboratory.

Nobel Prize

In 1977 Yalow received the Nobel Prize in Physiology or Medicine for her and Berson's development of RIA as it applied to tracing hormones in the body. Since Nobel Prizes are only given to the living, Yalow received the award without Berson, who died in 1972. She shared it with two other scientists, who were honoured for their work on hormone production in the brain.

Yalow named the lab at the VA hospital in the Bronx—which by 1972 was much larger than the janitor's closet where she had started out—for Berson so that his name would still be on every paper she published as long as she worked there.

In addition to receiving the Nobel Prize, she was the first woman to receive the Albert Lasker Basic Medical Research Award (1976), and in 1988 she was awarded the National Medal of Science by President Ronald Reagan. She continued to conduct and direct research at her VA lab until her retirement in 1991. Yalow was a distinguished service professor at Mount Sinai School of Medicine.

Rosalyn Yalow (Banquet Speech)

Rosalyn Yalow's speech at the Nobel Banquet, December 10, 1977

Your Majesties, Your Royal Highnesses, Ladies, Gentlemen and you, the students, who are the carriers of our hopes for the survival of the world and our dreams for its future. Tradition has ordained that one of the Laureates represent all of us in responding to your tribute. The choice of one among the several deemed truly and equally distinguished must indeed be difficult. Perhaps I have been selected for this privilege because there is certainly one way in which I am distinguishable from the others. This difference permits me to address myself first to a very special problem.

Among you Students of Stockholm and among other students, at least in the Western world, women are represented in reasonable proportion to their numbers in the community; yet among the scientists, scholars, and leaders of our world they are not. No objective testing has revealed such substantial differences in talent as to account for this discrepancy. The failure of women to have reached positions of leadership has been due in large part to social and professional discrimination. In the past, few women have tried and even fewer have succeeded. We still live in a world in which a significant fraction of people, including women, believe that a woman belongs and wants to belong exclusively in the home; that a woman should not aspire to achieve more than her male counterparts and particularly not more than her husband. Even now women with exceptional qualities for leadership sense from their parents, teachers, and peers that they must be harder-working, accomplish more and yet are less likely to receive appropriate rewards than are men. These are real problems which may never disappear or, at best, will change very slowly.

We cannot expect in the immediate future that all women who seek it will achieve full equality of opportunity. But if women are to start moving towards that goal, we must believe in ourselves or no one else will believe in us; we must match our aspirations with the competence, courage, and determination to succeed; and we must feel a personal responsibility to ease the path for those who come afterwards. The world cannot afford the loss of the talents of half its people if we are to solve the many problems which beset us.

If we are to have faith that mankind will survive and thrive on the face of the earth, we must believe that each succeeding generation will be wiser than its progenitors. We transmit to you, the next generation, the total sum of our knowledge. Yours is the responsibility to use it, add to it, and transmit it to your children.

A decade ago, during the period of world-wide student uprisings there was deep concern that too many of our young people were so disillusioned as to feel that the world must be destroyed before it could be rebuilt. Even now, it is all too easy to be pessimistic if we consider our multiple problems: the possible depletion of resources faster than science can generate replacements or substitutes; hostilities between nations and between groups within nations which appear not to be resolvable; unemployment and vast inequalities among different races and different lands. Even as we envision and solve scientific problems – and put men on the moon – we appear ill-equipped to provide solutions for the social ills that beset us.

We bequeath to you, the next generation, our knowledge but also our problems. While we still live, let us join hands, hearts, and minds to work together for their solution so that your world will be better than ours and the world of your children even better.

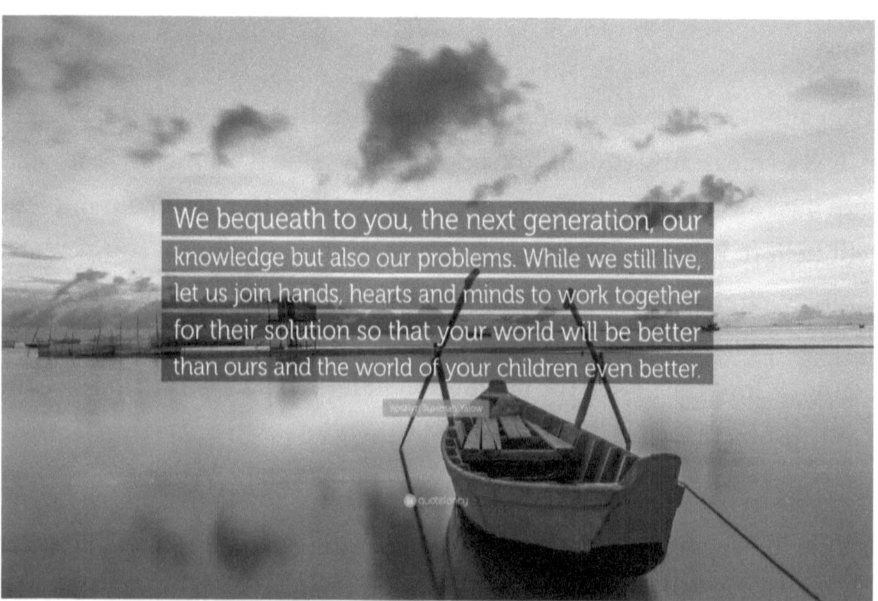

Fig. 27. Rosalyn Yalow indicates some direction and dependency on the future generation.

Extraordinary Drive

At a personal level, Yalow had extraordinary drive and a legendary capacity for work. Despite her commitment to her research, she strove to balance her career with family. She would frequently run home to prepare meals for her husband Aaron and their two children, Benjamin and Elanna, before returning to the laboratory. She shunned feminist organizations but was a forceful advocate for equal opportunities in science, and she was known to encourage high school girls to pursue scientific careers. Ultimately, she was a pioneering scientist and great intellect who without formal training in biology, helped unravel many mysteries of physiology and medicine.

Dream of Rosalyn Yalow

Solomon died of a heart attacked in 1972, and Rosalyn was devastated. She lost her best friends and her lab partner. Rosalyn realized she needed to prove herself now that she was a lone woman in the scientific sphere. She worked hard and published over 60 research articles in only 4 years. Rosalyn never gave up on her dream and kept a chilled bottle of champagne in her office every year in case she won the Nobel Prize. In 1977, that dream came true when she was awarded the Nobel Prize in Physiology or Medicine for her work in endocrinology.

We all face obstacles, and Rosalyn is a prime example of how we should not give up on chasing our dreams. In her own words, "we must believe in ourselves or no one else will believe in us; we must match our aspirations with the competence, courage, and determination to succeed."

Memorable Moment for Rosalyn Yalow

At 6: 45, the morning of October 13, 1977, Yalow was already at work in her study when the telephone rang. She had been awarded half of the Nobel Prize for Physiology or Medicine, "for the development of radioimmunoassay of peptide hormones." Unfortunately, Yalow's late co-worker Berson could not share with her the triumph of their long joint activity. The other half was shared jointly by Roger C. L. Guillemin of the Salk Institute and Dr. Andrew V. Schally of the Veterans Administration Hospital in New Orleans, who had researched brain hormones . Yalow became the first American-born woman to win the Nobel Prize in medicine and the second woman laureate in medicine, following Gerty Cori, who had been honoured in 1947.

Life After the Nobel Prize

After the excitement and publicity of the Nobel Prize, the tireless Yalow continued to work in her modest laboratory in the Bronx and remained in her home in nearby Riverdale, New York. She also served as chair of the department of clinical science at Bronx's Montefiore Hospital and Medical Center from 1980 to 1985. She collected a growing number of honorary degrees, including those from Yeshiva University—where she held the title of Distinguished Professor-at-Large emerita beginning in 1986—and Hunter College, her alma mater. In 1978, the Rosalyn S. Yalow Research Development Award was established. For the second time, she was given the VA Exceptional Service Award, then the Torch of Learning award by the American Friends of the Hebrew University. She even found time to host a five-part dramatic series for Public Broadcasting on the life of Marie Curie, one of Yalow's own early role models. Through it all, she refused to allow fame to change her lifestyle.

Yalow continued writing papers (a total of over 500) and doing research. In 1988, she was awarded the National Medal of Science and in 1993 she was inducted into the National Women's Hall of Fame.

Her Personality

As a woman, Rosalyn had to overcome many obstacles before being able to devote her life full-time to scientific research. However, being – in her own words – stubborn and single-minded since childhood, she did not give up and continued along the path she had chosen without a second thought.

Married to her colleague Aaron Yalow and a mother to two children, even after achieving success in her career, Rosalyn never stopped fighting against female discrimination. She strived for women to always be guaranteed equal opportunities in accessing education and was known to encourage young female students to pursue scientific careers.

When she was awarded the Nobel Prize, she said:

We cannot expect in the immediate future that all women who seek it will achieve full equality of opportunity. But if women are to start moving towards that goal, we must believe in ourselves or no one else will believe in us; we must match our aspirations with the competence, courage, and determination to succeed; and we must feel a personal responsibility to ease the path for those who come afterwards.

[Rosalyn Yalow]

End Point of the Life of Yalow

At age seventy-one, Yalow officially retired and became Senior Medical Investigator Emerita at the VA Hospital and the Solomon A. Berson distinguished professor-at-large at Mount Sinai School of Medicine in New York. She came to the lab several times a week and claimed to be still cooking dinners nightly for her husband, a physics professor at Cooper Union College in New York City. She continued to respond to mail, give interviews, and help students at the VA's Berson laboratory. Her husband, Dr. Aaron Yalow died in 1992, at the age of 72, from cardiac arrest.

Over the course of the 1990s, Yalow suffered from a series of strokes. In 1997 while rehabilitating at the Hebrew Home in Bronx, New York, she was invited to speak at the institution's "Take Your Daughter to Work Day." She told the audience of girls, "It was a delight to win the Nobel Prize, but it gave me a responsibility to see that women become more interested in working in science and that they are able to work at a level that will allow them to achieve their maximum potential." Yalow recuperated from this stroke and was able to return to her lab. She continued to respond to mail from students and give brief interviews until she died on May 30, 2011, at the age of 89. Yalow defied gender and religious barriers in the field of science and made breakthrough discoveries that changed the field of medicine.

Fig. 28. Rosalyn Yalow at her desk at the VA Medical Centre in Bronx, New York

Medical Giant, Medical Victim

It happened four years after Yalow's mandatory retirement from the VA hospital at the age of 70 and three years since the passing of her husband.

She was rushed by ambulance to a nearby university hospital. She had lectured there on several occasions, and the university had awarded her an honorary degree. ***"The house officer in the emergency room didn't remember her name,"*** recalled Yalow's friend and fellow physician Eugene Straus. ***"But he remembered a rather dirty old lady who had suffered a stroke. They refused to admit her...she had been 'dumped.'"*** The Nobel Prize-winning scientist, unconscious and unrecognized after suffering an ischemic stroke, was then transferred to a second hospital for admission. Yalow regained consciousness after five days and left the hospital two weeks later. She would go on to live until **the age of 90, dying on 30 May, 2011.**

Nobel Laureates, Women, and Diabetes Discoveries

Fig. 29. Gerty Cori (left) and Rosalyn Yalow (right)

What does the first woman to receive the Nobel Prize in Physiology or Medicine say to the second?

It took 30 years, but I'm no longer the only one!

That would be Gerty Cori, M. D., a biochemist, saying it to Rosalyn Yalow, Ph. D., a physicist.

Cori would win the Nobel in 1947, with her husband, for discoveries related to how the body metabolizes sugars, showing that glycogen—a derivative of glucose—is broken down and used as a source of energy. They also found that insulin causes the removal of sugar from the blood. Their discoveries formed the foundation for later work in the management of diabetes.

Yalow would receive the Prize in 1977, for discovering a technique, using insulin, to detect trifling amounts of any protein with a radioactive assay, called a radioimmunoassay.

Published March 23, 2021 in Life with T1D, Research

Comments of Professor Shimon Glick

(He was a research fellow and then a clinical investigator in Berson and Yalow's laboratory from 1961 to 1964.)

When Berson died in 1972 at the age of 53, Rosalyn was devastated. Many who did not know her well suspected that he was the 'brains' and she the 'muscle.' She disproved the doubters: between Berson's death and her receiving the Nobel Prize in Physiology or Medicine (with medical scientists Roger Guillemin and Andrew Schally), she published dozens of important papers on the structure and function of various hormones.

Shimon Glick was professor emeritus at the Faculty of HealthSciences of Ben Gurion Universityof the Negev, Beer Sheva,84105 Israel.

e-mail: gshimon@bgu.ac.il

Ursula B. Kaiser, MD

Harvard Medical School

Chief, Division of Endocrinology,Diabetesand Hypertension

Endocrine Society president Ursula B. Kaiser, MD, chief of the Division of Endocrinology, Diabetes, and Hypertension; George W. Thorn, MD, Distinguished Chair in Endocrinology; and director of the Brigham Research Institute at Brigham and Women's Hospital, as well as professor of medicine at Harvard Medical School, Boston, Mass., says that it was Yalow's radioimmunoassays that allowed Drs. Guillemin and Schally to purify and isolate hypothalamic neuropeptides such as GnRH (also known as LHRH). "Dr. Yalow had a tremendous influence on my career," Kaiser says. "My research focus during my fellowship was on how varying frequencies of pulsatile GnRH differentially regulated LH and FSH, based in large part on the work of Drs. Yalow, Schally and Guillemin, and the subsequent elegant studies of pulsatile GnRH done by Ernst Knobil. Dr. Yalow was also a tremendous role model for women in science!"

(N. B.: Endocrine Society members have elected Ursula B. Kaiser, MD, to serve as the organization's President for the 2022–2023 term).

Why Remember Rosalyn Sussman

There are all reasons why Rosalyn should be remembered now and in generations to come. First, Rosalyn was a successful teacher, mother, and wife. She is the epitome of how one can mix both education and motherhood and still become successful in both. This is contrary to contemporary women who will forego one to perfect the other. However, even if we do not remember Rosalyn for her rare abilities in balancing motherhood and education, we cannot fail to remember her for the contribution she made in immunology. The invention of RIA was a landmark achievement in immunology not forgetting that it is a woman who achieved it. Today we can determine levels of insulin among other biological components in the body. The invention of RIA brought a revolution in the medical world. Actually, some of her critics, who rejected her two first journals on radioimmunoassay, came to embrace her findings later in life.

Rosalyn broke conventions and proved that women are not lesser beings and they can do more than staying back at home to look after children and carry out household chores. We should remember Rosalyn for her outstanding achievements in representing women in the scientific arena. After her retirement, this heroine did not go to relax and enjoy her wealth and fame. She used her status to campaign for children's rights (CWP and Regents of the University of California). We will remember this mother, wife, scientist, and activist as an epitome of audacity and hope. Today women can venture into science fearlessly with the firm belief that someone somewhere made it. This is none other than one Rosalyn Sussman Yalow. She is a true champion and mentioning RIA without Rosalyn will be nothing short of discredit.

Insights from Rosalyn

In the wake of reading Rosalyn's story, the writer realized that all things are possible. If Rosalyn made it in science, managed to emerge as the first woman to venture into science and succeed, then anyone can do what he or she wants to be provided there is desire, resources, opportunities, and hard work.

Conclusion

Working out of an old janitor's closet for a laboratory, two researchers at a Veterans Administration (VA) hospital in the Bronx, New York, developed the technique in the late 1950s. They were Rosalyn Yalow (1921–2011) and Solomon A. Berson (1918–1972). The most important technique is known as Radioimmunoassay (RIA). It is a technique that uses radioactive materials to investigate the human body for tiny amounts of substances. Yalow received the Nobel Prize in Physiology or Medicine (in 1977) for her and Berson's development of RIA as it applied to tracing hormones in the body. Since Nobel Prizes are only given to the living, Yalow received the award without Berson, who died in 1972.

Rosalyn Sussman Yalow became the first woman, born in America to win the coveted Nobel Prize in science. She has travelled a long way to be where she is today. She dared to venture into physics even though men dominated this field hitherto. She is the co-inventor of RIA; a method that is being used world all over in laboratories to detect biological components in blood. Interestingly, Rosalyn believes that her success comes from within and she has no place for God or religion per se.

Rosalyn Yalow lived nearly all of her life in the Bronx, where she was born, educated, and worked, raised her family, and met Solomon Berson, her scientific partner for many years. Yalow and Berson were born in New York, children, and grandchildren of immigrants from Europe. Both of their families' finances were constrained due to shortage of capital, anti-Semitic impediments to employment, and the Great Depression.

Both Berson and Yalow were educated in New York City public schools. Berson graduated from the legendary City College of New York, then all-male and tuition-free. After graduation, it took him three years (earning a master's degree and working as an assistant in the New York University Anatomy Department) before he broke through the extreme barriers then in place for Jewish applicants to medical school. Berson bragged about his hundred or more medical school rejections.

Yalow was a top student at Hunter College, the tuition-free, all-female counterpart of City College, where she majored in physics. Despite a brilliant record, she failed to gain admission to any graduate programs in physics, specifically and openly because she was female and Jewish. Finally, as a favour to one of her Hunter College professors, the University of Illinois accepted her into their PhD program in nuclear physics with the condition that they bear no responsibility for placing her in a job after graduation. Indeed, despite a brilliant school record and the World War II shortage of civilian males, employment for her was spotty. It was two years before she joined the Veterans Administration Hospital ("Bronx VA") as a consultant and five years until she was hired as a full-time physicist.

In 1950, Yalow met and recruited Dr. Solomon Berson, a talented resident physician at her workplace. She was impressed by his strong personality and background, which was similar to hers. Rosalyn gave up on working with other scientists to focus on her work with Dr. Berson. Together, they would form a strong working relationship in developing the radioimmunoassay (RIA) technique. Their work relationship was a perfect match, and they shared the credits in every achievement. Yalow and Berson began a research partnership that was to last 22 years, until Berson's untimely death in 1972.

Together, Yalow and Berson tore through hormone research, interpreting their discovery of RIA as a starting gun. What they learned allowed researchers to tell the difference between patients with type 1 and type 2 diabetes; which children would be able to benefit from human growth hormone treatments; whether ulcers should be operated on or handled with medication; which newborns needed a medical intervention for underactive thyroid…and the list goes on. Though others were slow to catch on, within a decade, the RIA technique energized scientists, transforming endocrinology into the "it" specialty in medical research. For eighteen years, Yalow and Berson knocked out hormone after hormone, furiously preparing solutions and loading 2,000 to 3,000 test tubes in twenty-four-hour stretches.

This was the first real proof that so small a protein could stimulate an immunologic response. The scientific establishment was reluctant to accept such a finding, and the two researchers had difficulty publishing their paper. The results were eventually published in 1959, and when their observations were confirmed by others, the significance of the discovery was clear. Not only had they proven that the human immune system could recognize and respond to smaller molecules than previously thought possible, but they had done so using a breakthrough technology.

Yalow and Berson called their method radioimmunoassay—the first technique to use radio isotopic techniques for the study of the primary reaction of antigen with antibody. Yalow and Berson had provided a means to observe the previously invisible world of antigen – antibody reactions that take place in solution. Before their ideas and methods, scientists were restricted in the analysis of reactions between antigens and antibodies to those that produced visible precipitation or other evidence, such as the clumping of red blood cells. The development of RIA stimulated a revolution in theoretical immunology and, in point of fact, all biology.

The RIA diagnostic process was, and continues to be, used by researchers in myriad ways. RIA is remarkably sensitive. It measures incredibly low concentrations of many substances. Adaptations of the RIA principle is also possible. Nonradioactive labels, such as linked enzymes and fluorescent markers, can be used in place of radioisotopes. Because of its almost limitless applicability, the RIA concept has spawned innumerable innovations in basic research and practical applications.

The commercial possibilities for RIA were enormous, but while Yalow and Berson recognized this, they refused to patent the method. Instead, they made every effort to get RIA into common use, putting its value to humanity ahead of their own financial interests. Indeed, Yalow and Berson performed all their work without ever receiving a research grant! This stands in sharp contrast to much contemporary medical research, which is corporate-sponsored and profit-oriented in the quest for intellectual property.

In 1968, Rosalyn Yalow became acting chief of the Radioisotope Service at the Bronx VA, when Berson left to become chair of the department of medicine at the Mount Sinai School of Medicine in New York. She assumed leadership of the RIA reference laboratory in 1969 and was the head of the nuclear medicine service from 1970 to 1980. Berson died of a heart attack in 1972, and although Yalow was grief-stricken, she continued to work; her laboratory published 60 articles between 1972 and 1976. She was elected to the National Academy of Sciences in 1975, and in the next year became the first woman to be awarded the Albert Lasker Prize for Basic Medical Research. Although extremely prestigious in its own right, the Lasker Prize is generally considered a precursor to the Nobel Prize in Physiology or Medicine. And true to form, in 1977 Yalow received the Nobel for her work on RIA. Her only regret was that Berson was not alive to share it with her.

In 1977, Yalow was the sixth individual woman (seventh overall, consideringMarie Curie's two wins), and first American-born woman, to win the Nobel Prize in a scientific field. She was also the second woman in the world to win in the physiology or medicine category (the first wasGerty Cori). Yalow was honoured for her role in devising the radioimmunoassay technique, along with Roger Guillemin and Andrew V. Schally for their research in another field.

Among Yalow's personality characteristics were her firm belief that a woman could do a good job in her chosen profession and still be an attentive mother. She was also an ardent campaigner for equal rights for women and was most adamant that person be recognized for their accomplishments, and not for their gender.

Even as she became a famed researcher, Yalow held fast in her beliefs that women should fulfil traditional roles at home. … She wrote, "All women scientists should marry, rear children, cook, and clean in order to achieve fulfilment, to be a complete woman."

In 1991, Yalow retired from the VA hospital at age 70. Since the death of her husband, Aaron, on August 8, 1992, her work has concentrated on formulating science policy. Yalow still frequented her laboratory, where she assisted postdoctoral fellows who came fromThird Worldnations to study. A motherly mentor, she attended professional presentations by her former students and followed their careers, and she proudly told of how many of her "professional children" had improved public health in their native lands.

At the same time, she asserted her motto, "We must believe in ourselves or no one will believe in us." In her Nobel speech she noted, "We still live in a world in which a significant fraction of people, including women, believe that a woman belongs—and wants to belong—exclusively in the home." Commenting that women are discouraged from achieving more than men, Yalow concluded, "we must match our aspirations with the competence, courage and determination to succeed, and we must feel a personal responsibility to ease the path for those who come afterward.... The world cannot afford the loss of the talents of half of its people if we are to solve the many problems which beset us."

In concluding her acceptance speech, Yalow pointed out that "the first telescope opened the heavens; the first microscope opened the world of microbes; radio isotopic methodology, as exemplified by RIA, has shown the potential for opening new vistas in science and medicine."

The author of this book expresses his respect and admiration in representing the dedication, perseverance, talent, and hard work of a Jewish women scientist for the discovery of an authentic technique, the RIA (**radioimmunoassay**) in the field of Physiology or Medicine for its innumerable innovations in basic research and practical applications.

Fig.30. Yalow and one of the guinea pigs whose antibodies made Radioimmunoassay possible

Fig. 31. Dr. Rosalyn Yalow at her Bronx Veterans Administration Hospital, Oct. 13, 1977, after learning she had won the Nobel Prize.

The Nobel Prize in Physiology or Medicine 1977

"for their discoveries concerning the peptide hormone production of the brain"

"For her development of radioimmunoassays of peptide hormones."

Roger Guillemin   **Andrew V. Schally**   **Rosalyn Yalow**

Fig. 32. The Nobel Prize in Physiology or Medicine 1977 was divided, one half jointly to Roger Guillemin, and Andrew V. Schally, "for their discoveries concerning the peptide hormone production of the brain" and the other half to Rosalyn Yalow "for the development of radioimmunoassay of peptide hormones."

References

Anderson, R. J. (2017)."Breaking Barriers: The Life and Work of Rosalyn Yalow"(PDF). The Pharmacologist;59(3): 152–163.

Barakat, R. S. and R. P. Ekins. (1961). "Assay of Vitamin B12 in Blood." Lancet; 2: 25–26.

Berson, S. A., Yalow, R. S., Bauman, A., Rothschild, M. A., Newerly, K. (1956). Insulin-I131 metabolism in human subjects: Demonstration of insulin binding globulin in the circulation of insulin treated subjects. J Clin Invest.; 35: 170 –190.

Berson, S. A. and R. S. Yalow. (1957). "Kinetics of Reaction Between Insulin and Insulin-Binding Antibody." J. Clin. Invest.; 36: 873.

Berson, S. A. (1957). Resume of Conference on Insulin Activity in Blood and Tissue Fluids. Editors: R. Levine and E. Anderson. National Institutes of Health, Bethesda, Maryland. p. 7.

Berson, S. A. and R. S. Yalow. (1958). "Isotopic tracers in the study of diabetes." Advances in Biological and Medical Physics. Academic Press. pp. 349–430.

Berson, S. A. and R. S. Yalow. (1959). "Species-Specificity of Human Anti-Beef Pork Insulin Serum." J. Clin. Invest.;38: 20–17–2025.

Berson, S. A., and Yalow, R. S. (1959). Quantitative aspects of the reaction between insulin and insulin binding antibody: relation to problem of insulin resistance. *J Clin Invest.*; 38: 1 996 –2016.

Berson, S. A. and R. S. Yalow. (1968). "Immunochemical Heterogeneity of Parathyroid Hormone in Plasma." J. Clin. Endocrinol. Metab.; 28: 1037–1047.

Berson, S. A. and R. S. Yalow. (1971). "Nature of Immunoreactive Gastrin Extracted from Tissues of Gastrointestinal Tract." Gastroenterology; 60: 215–222.

Berson, S. A., J. H. Walsh, and R. S. Yalow. (1973). Frontiers in Gastrointestinal Hormone Research. Almqvist & Wiksell, Stockholm. pp. 57–66.

Bloomsbury Publishing Plc,Fitzhenry & Whiteside, Limited (1996). Who's who 1996: An Annual Biographical Dictionary, *Who's Who Series*, A & C Black Publisher, 1996,

Brownstein, M., A. Arimura, H. Sato, A. V. Schally and J. S. Kizer. (1975). "The Regional Distribution of Somatostatin in the Rat Brain." Endocrinology; 96: 1456–1461.

Bryant, M. G., J. M. Polak, I. Modlin, S. R. Bloom, R. H. Alburquerque and A. G. E. Pearse. (1976). "Possible Dual Role for Vasoactive Intestinal Peptide as Gastrointestinal Hormone and Neurotransmittal Substance." Lancet;1: 991–993.

Cheung, A. L. and A. Goldstein. (1976). "Failure of Hypophysectomy to Alter Brain Content of Opioid Peptides (Endorphins)." Life Sci.; 19: 1005–1008.

Chopra, I. J., David, H. S., and Gildon N. B. (1971). "Radioimmunoassay for Measurement of Triiodothyronine in Human Serum. *Journal of Clinical Investigation*; 50: 203341.

Cohn, D. V., R. R. MacGregor, L. L. H. Chu, J. R. Kimmel, and J. W. Hamilton. (1972). "Calcemic Fraction-A: Biosynthetic Peptide Precursor of Parathyroid Hormone." Proc. Nat. Acad. Sci.; 69: 1521–1525.

Day, E. D. (1966). Foundations of Immunochemistry. Williams and Wilkins Co.

Dockray, G. J. (1976). "Immunochemical Evidence of Cholecystokinin-like Peptides in Brain." Nature; 264: 568–570.

Ekins, R. P. (1960). "The Estimation of Thyroxine in Human Plasma by an Electrophoretic Technique." Clin. Chim. Acta; 5: 453–459.

Gellene, D. (2011). "Rosalyn S. Yalow, Nobel Medical Physicist, Dies at 89". The New York Times. p. B18. Retrieved October 8 , 2020.

Gibbs, J., R. C. Young and G. P. Smith. (1973). "Cholecystokinin Elicits Satiety in Rats with Open Gastrics Fistula." Nature; 245: 323–325.

Gibbs, J., R. C. Young and G. P. Smith. (1973). "Cholecystokinin Decreases Food Intake in Rats." J. Comp. Physiol. Psychol.; 84: 488–495.

Glick, S. M., Roth, J., Yalow, R. S., Berson, S. A. (1965). The regulation of growth hormone secretion. *Recent ProgHorm Res.*; 21: 241–283.

Glick, S. (2011). "Rosalyn Sussman Yalow (1921–2011): The second woman to win the Nobel prize in medicine". Nature.; 474: 580.doi: 10.1038/474580a. PMID21720355.

Goldsmith, S. J. (1987). "Georg de Hevesy Nuclear Medicine Pioneer Award Citation--1986. Rosalyn S. Yalow and Solomon A. Berson",J. Nucl. Med.;28(10): 1637–9, PMID3309206

Gregory, R. A., and H. J. Tracy. (1964). "The Constitution and Properties of Two Gastrins Extracted from Hog Antral Mucosa: I. The Isolation of Two Gastrins from Hog Antral Mucosa." Gut; 5: 103–114.

Gregory, R. A., H. J. Tracy, and M. I. Grossman. (1966). "Isolation of Two Gastrins from Human Antral Mucosa." Nature; 209: 583.

Gregory, R. A., and H. J. Tracy. (1972). "Isolation of Two 'Big Gastrins' from Zollinger-Ellison Tumour Tissue." Lancet; 2: 797–799.

Gregory, R. A., and H. J. Tracy. (1973). "Big Gastrin." Mt. Sinai J. Med.; 40: 359–364.

Haber, L. (1979). Women Pioneers of Science. New York: Harcourt Brace Jovanovich. ISBN.

Harrod, J. (2019)."Meet Rosalyn Sussman Yalow, the first American-born woman to win a Nobel Prize, who let doctors see into your blood". Massive Science. Retrieved 2019-06-20.

Hays, M. H. (2010). "A historical look at the establishment of the Department of Veterans Affairs Research & Development Program"(PDF). U. S. Government Publishing Office. Department of Veterans Affairs Research & Development Program. Retrieved 2016–10–02.

Herbert, V. (1959). "Studies on the Role of Intrinsic Factor in Vitamin B12 Absorption, Transport and Storage." Am. J. Clin. Nutr.; 7: 433–443

Herbert, V., Z. Castro, and L. R. Wasserman. (1960). "Stoichiometric Relation Between Liver-Receptor, Intrinsic Factor and Vitamin B12." Proc. Soc. Exp. Biol. Med.; 104: 160–164.

Hokfelt, T., S. Efendic, C. Hellerstrom, O. Johansson, R. Luft, and A. Arimura. (1975). "Cellular Localization of Somatostatin in Endocrine-like Cells and Neurons of the Rat with Special References to the A1-Cells of the Pancreatic Islets and to the Hypothalamus." Acta Endocrinol.; 80 (Suppl. 200): 1–41.

Hong, J. S., T. Yang, W. Fratta and E. Costa. (1977). "Determination of Methionine Enkephalin in Discrete Regions of Rat Brain." Brain Res.;134: 383–386.

Howes, R. H.(2011)."Rosalyn Sussman Yalow (1921–2011)". Physics & Society;40(4).

Jorpes, J. E. and V. Mutt. (1973). Methods in Investigative and Diagnostic Endocrinology, Part III – Non-Pituitary Hormones. Editors: S. A. Person and R. S. Yalow. North-Holland Publishing Co., Amsterdam. pp. 1075–1080.

Kahn, C. R., Roth, J. (2004). Berson, Yalow, and the JCI: the agony and the ecstasy. *J Clin Invest.*; 114(8): 1051–1054.

Kahn, C. R., Roth, J. (2012). "Rosalyn Sussman Yalow (1921–2011)". Proceedings of the National Academy of Sciences of the United States of America.; 109(3): 669–670.

Kemper, B., J. F. Habener, J. T. Potts, Jr., and A. Rich. (1972). "Proparathyroid Hormone: Identification of a Biosynthetic Precursor to Parathyroid Hormone." Proc. Nat. Acad. Sci.; 69: 643–647.

Krieger, D. T., A. Liotta, and M. J. Brownstein. (1977). "Presence of Corticotropin in Brain of Normal and Hypophysectomised Rats." Proc. Nat. Acad. Sci.; 74: 648–652.

Krieger, D. T., A. Liotta, and M. J. Brownstein. (1977). "Presence of Corticotropin in Limbic System of Normal and Hypophysectomised Rats." Brain Res.; 128: 575–579.

Kyle, R. A., Shampo, M. A. (2002). "Rosalyn Yalow--pioneer in nuclear medicine", Mayo Clin. Proc.;77 (1): 4.

Lazarus, N. R., J. E. Panhos, T. Tanese, L. Michaels, R. Gutman and L. Recant. (1970). "Studies on the Biological Activity of Porcine Proinsulin." J. Clin. Invest.; 49: 487.

Leeman, S. E., E. A. Mroz and R. E. Carraway. (1977). Peptides in Neurobiology. Editor: H. Gainer. Plenum Press, New York. pp. 99–144.

McGrayne, S. B. (1998). Rosalyn Sussman Yalow. *Nobel Prize Women in Science.* (pp. 332–354). Washington, DC: Joseph Henry Press.

Miner R. W., ed. (1944). Transactions Of The New York Academy of Sciences. Vol.7. p.168. Retrieved October 8, 2020.

Mirsky, I. A. (1952). "The Etiology of Diabetes Mellitus in Man." Recent Progr. Horm. Res.; 7: 437.

Moldow, R. and R. S. Yalow. (1978). "Extrahypophysial Distribution of Corticotropin as a Function of Brain Size." Proc. Nat. Acad. Sci.; 75: 997–998.

Muller, J. E, E. Straus, and R. S. Yalow. (1977). "Cholecystokinin and Its C-terminal Octapeptide in the Pig Brain." Proc. Nat. Acad. Sci.; 74: 3035–3037.

Murphy, B. E. P. (1964). "Application of the Property of Protein-Binding to the Assay of Minute Quantities of Hormones and Other Substances." Nature (Lond.); 201: 679–682.

Newerly, K., Berson, S. A. (1957). Lack of specificity of insulin-I 131 – binding by isolated rat diaphragm. Proc. Soc. Exp. Biol. Med.; 94: 751–755.

Opfell, O. S. (1978). The Lady Laureates: Women Who Have Won the Nobel Prize. Metuchen, N. J & London: Scarecrow Press, Inc. pp.224–233. ISBN.

Patton, D. D. (2002). "Three Nobelists who paved the way", J. Nucl. Med.; 43(3): 25N–28N.

Raju, T. N. (1999). "The Nobel chronicles. 1977: Roger Charles Louis Guillemin (b 1924); Andrew Victor Schally (b 1926); Rosalyn S Yalow (b 1921)",Lancet; 354(9188): 1481.

Rall, J. E. (1990). "Solomon A. Berson: 1918–1972." In Biographical Memoirs. Washington, D. C.: National Academy of Sciences.

Roth J. Solomon A. Berson. (1973). Diabetes; 22(1) : 66–68.

Roth J. (1973). Peptide hormone binding to receptors: a review of direct studies in vitro. Metabolism.; 22(8): 1059–1073.

Roth J, Taylor SI. (1982). Information transfer cell regulation and disease mechanism: insights from studies of cell surface receptors. Harvey Lect.; 77: 81–127.

Rothenberg, S. P. (1961). "Assay of Serum Vitamin B12Concentration Using Co57-B12and Intrinsic Factor." Proc. Soc. Exp. Biol. Med.; 108: 45–48.

Samols, E. (1979). "Solomon A. Berson—A Brief Biography." Seminars in Nuclear Medicine; 9: 1737.

Saxena, B. B., Hiroshi, D., Hortense, M. G., and Ralph, E. P. (1968). "Radioimmunoassay of Human Follicle Stimulating and Luteinizing Hormones in Plasma."Journal of Clinical Endocrinology and Metabolism; 28: 51934.

Schally, A. V., T. W. Redding, H. W. Lucien, and J. Meyer. (1967). "Enterogastrone Inhibits Eating by Fasted Mice." Science; 157: 210–211.

Schwartz, I. L. (1973). "Solomon A. Berson and Rosalyn S. Yalow: a scientific appreciation", Mt. Sinai J. Med.; 40(3): 284–94.

Silverman, R., and R. S. Yalow. (1973). "Heterogeneity of Parathyroid Hormone: Clinical and Physiologic Implications." J. Clin. Invest.; 52: 1958–1971.

Simantov, R., M. J. Kuhar, G. R. Uhl and S. H. Snyder. (1977). "Opioid Peptide Enkephalin: Immunohistochemical Mapping in Rat Central Nervous System." Proc. Nat. Acad. Sci.; 74: 2167–2171.

Steiner, D. F., D. Cunningham, L. Spigelman and B. Aten. (1967). "Insulin Biosynthesis: Evidence for a Precursor." Science; 157: 697.

Steiner, D. F., J. L. Clark, C. Nolan, A. H. Rubenstein, E. Margoliash, F. Melani and P. E. Oyer. (1970). Pathogenesis of Diabetes Mellitus. Nobel Symposium 13. Editors: E. Cerasi and R. Luft. Almqvist & Wiksell, Stockholm, Sweden. pp. 57–78.

Straus, E., and R. S. Yalow. (1974). "Studies on the Distribution and Degradation of Heptadecapeptide, Big, and Big Gastrin." Gastroenterology; 66: 936–943.

Straus, E., and R. S. Yalow. (1975). Gastrointestinal Hormones. Editor: J. C. Thompson. Unvi. Texas Press, Austin. pp. 99–113.

Straus. E. and R. S. Yalow. (1977). "Radioimmunoassay for Tuberculin Purified Protein Derivative." Clin. Res.; 25: A384.

Straus, E., J. E. Muller, H-S. Choi, F. Paronetto and R. S Yalow. (1977). "Immunohistochemical Localization in Rabbit Brain of a peptide Resembling the C-terminal Cholecystokinin Octapeptide." Proc. Nat. Acad. Sci.; 74: 3033–3034.

Straus, E., and R. S. Yalow. (1978). "Species Specificity of Cholecystokinin in Gut and Brain of Several Mammalian Species." Proc. Nat. Acad. Sci.; 75: 486–489.

Straus, E. W. (1992). "Festschrift for Rosalyn S. Yalow: Hormones, metabolism, and society", Mt. Sinai J. Med.; 59 (2): 95–100.

Straus E. (1998). Rosalyn Yalow, Nobel Laureate: Her Life and Work in Medicine: A Biographical Memoir. New York: Plenum Trade;.[Google Scholar]

Straus, E. (1999). Rosalyn Yalow, Nobel Laureate: Her Life and Work in Medicine. Cambridge, MA: Perseus Books. ISBN

Straus, E. (2000). " Rosalyn Yalow: Nobel Laureate: Her Life and Work in Medicine ", Medical Physics, Basic Books; 26(4): 222–223.

Taitz, E., and Sondra, H. (1996). Remarkable Jewish Women: Rebels, Rabbis, and Other Women in History from Biblical Times to the Present. Philadelphia: Jewish Publication Society.

Topley, W. W. C. and G. S. Wilson. (1941). The Principles of Bacteriology and Immunity. Williams and Wilkins Co.

Unnikrishnan, A. G. (2011). "The Other Insulin Story of 1921". Indian Journal of Endocrinology and Metabolism.; 15(3): 147–148.

Vanderhaeghen, J. J., J. C. Signeau and W. Gepts. (1975). "New Peptide in the A Vertebrate CNS Reacting with Antigastrin Antibodies." Nature; 257: 604–605.

Who's Who (1996).

Walsh, J. H., Yalow, R. S., and Berson, S. A. (1970). Radioimmunoassay of Australia antigen. Vox Sang.; 19(3): 217–224.

Walsh, J. H., H. T. Debas and M. I. Grossman. (1974). "Pure Human Big Gastrin: Immunochemical Properties, Disappearance Half-Time, and Acid-Stimulating Action in Dogs." J. Clin. Invest.; 54: 477–485.

Yalow, R. S. and S. A. Berson. (1959). "Assay of Plasma Insulin in Human Subjects by Immunological Methods." Nature; 184: 1648–1649.

Yalow, R. S. and S. A. Berson. (1960). "Immunoassay of Endogenous Plasma Insulin in Man." J. Clin. Invest.; 39: 1157–1175.

Yalow, R. S., Glick, S. M., Roth, J., Berson, S. A. (1964). Radioimmunoassay of human plasma ACTH. J Clin Endocrinol Metab.; 24: 1219–1225.

Yalow, R. S. and S. A. Berson. (1970). "Size and Charge Distinctions Between Endogenous Human Plasma Gastrin in Peripheral Blood and Heptadecapeptide Ga223strins." Gastroenterology; 58: 609–615.

Yalow, R. S. and S. A. Berson. (1970). "Radioimmunoassay of Gastrin." Gastroenterology; 58: 1–14.

Yalow, R. S. and S. A. Berson. (1971). "Further Studies on the Nature of Immunoreactive Gastrin in Human Plasma." Gastroenterology; 60: 203–214.

Yalow, R. S. and S. A. Berson. (1971). "Size Heterogeneity of Immunoreactive Human ACTH in Plasma and in Extracts of Pituitary Glands and ACTH-Producing Thymoma." Biochem. Biophys. Res. Commun.; 44: 439–445.

Yalow, R. S. and S. A Berson. (1973). "Characteristics of 'big ACTH' in Human Plasma and Pituitary Extracts." J. Clin. Endocrinol. Metab.; 36: 415–423.

Yalow, R. S. and L. Gross. (1976). "Radioimmunoassay for Intact Gross Mouse Leukemia Virus." Proc. Nat. Acad. Sci.; 73: 2847–2851.

Yalow, R. S. (1977)."Autobiography". Nobelprize.org. Retrieved October 2, 2012.

Yalow, R. S. (1977). Radioimmunoassay: A probe for fine structure of biologic systems. In: Lindsten J, editor. Nobel Lectures, Physiology or Medicine 1971–1980. Teaneck,NJ: World Scientific; 1977. pp. 447–468.[Google Scholar]

Yalow, R. S. (1978). Radioimmunoassay: a probe for the fine structure of biologic systems (Nobel Lecture, 8 December1977). *Science.*; 200 (4347): 1236–1245.

Yalow, R. S. (1984). Radioimmunoassay in Oncology, Cancer; 53: 1426 – 1431.

Yalow, R. S. (1992). "The Nobel lectures in immunology. The Nobel Prize for Physiology or Medicine, 1977 awarded to Rosalyn S. Yalow", Scand. J. Immunol.; 35 (1): 1–23.

Yalow, R. S., Berson, S. A. (1996). "Immunoassay of endogenous plasma insulin in man. 1960", Obes. Res.; 4(6): 583–600.

Yanaihara, N. (1978). "1977 Nobel Prize winners in medicine and physiology", Tanpakushitsu Kakusan Koso; 23(3) : 232–6, PMID 349610

Zucker, B. (1976). Laboratory Management. The Medical Div. of the United Business Publications, Inc. pp. 35–38.

Suggested Reading

Gleasner, Diana C. *Breakthrough: Women in Science.* NY: Walker, 1983.

Opfell, Olga S. *The Lady Laureates: Women Who Have Won the Nobel Prize.* Metuchen, NJ: Scarecrow, 1978.

Rall, J. Edward. "Solomon A. Berson," in *Biographical Memoirs of the National Academy of Sciences.* Washington, DC: National Academy Press, 1990.

Rayner, William P. *Wise Women: Singular Lives That Helped Shape Our Century.* NY: St. Martin's, 1983.

Straus, Eugene. *Rosalyn Yalow, Nobel Laureate: Her Life and Work in Medicine.* Plenum, 1998.

Bibliography

American Jewish Biographies Facts on File, 1982.

Contributions of 20th Century Women to Physics. University of California, 2001.

Current Biography. Bronx: H. W. Wilson Co., 1978.

Dash, Joan. The Triumph of Discovery: Women Scientists Who Won the Nobel Prize. Englewood Cliffs, NJ: Julian Messner, 1991.

EJ (1973–1982).

Gellene, Denise. "Rosalyn S. Yalow, Nobel Medical Physicist, Dies at 89." The New York Times, June 2, 2011,www.nytimes.com/2011/06/02/us/02yalow.html.

Glick S. (2011) Rosalyn Sussman Yalow (1921–2011). Nature 474(7353): 580

Kahn R. C. and Ross J. (2012) Rosalyn Sussman Yalow (1921–2011). Proceedings of the National Academy of Sciences of the United States of America 109(3): 669–670

Les Prix Nobel. Stockholm: Almqvist & Wiksell International, 1977.

McGrayne S. B. (1993) Rosalyn Sussman Yalow. In Nobel Prize Women in Science. Their Lives, Struggles, and Momentous Discoveries, Carol Publishing Group, pp. 333–355

MIT Inventor of the Week Archive (1999).

Opfell O. S. (1986) A sensitive Measure. Rosalyn Yalow. In The Lady Laureates. Women who have won the Nobel Prize, The Scarecrow Press, Inc., Metuchen, N. J., and London, pp. 254–264

The Scientist 11 (14): 1 (July 7, 1997).

Straus E. (1998) Rosalyn Yalow, Nobel Laureate: Her Life and Work in Medicine: A Biographical Memoir (Plenum, New York)

Ross J. (2011) A tribute to Rosalyn S. Yalow. The Journal of Clinical Investigation 121(8): 2949–2951

Sussman Yalow R. (1977) Radioimmunoassay: A probe for the fine structure of biologic systems. Nobel Lecture, December 1977, http://www.nobelprize.org/nobel_prizes/medicine/laureates/1977/yalow-lecture.pdf

Taitz, Emily, and Sondra Henry. Remarkable Jewish Women: Rebels, Rabbis, and Other Women in History from Biblical Times to the Present. Philadelphia: Jewish Publication Society, 1996.

Walsh, J. H., R. S. Yalow and S. A. Berson. 1970. "Radioimmunoassay of Australia Antigen." Vox Sanguins 19, 217–224.

Walsh, J. H., R. S. Yalow and S. A. Berson. 1970. "Detection of Australia Antigen and Antibody by Means of Radioimmunoassay Techniques." J. Inf. Dis.; 121, 550–554.

Wasson T. (ed.) (1987) Yalow, Rosalyn S. In Nobel Prize Winners, H. W. Wilson Company, New York, pp. 1148–1150

Who's Who(1996).

Some Important Publications

"Radioimmunoassay: A Probe for the Fine Structure of Biological Systems", Science 200: 1236 (1978) – – Nobel Prize Lecture.

S. A. Berson, R. S. Yalow, A. Bauman, M. A. Rothschild, and K. Newerly (1956). "Insulin-I131 Metabolism in Human Subjects: Demonstration of Insulin Binding Globulin in the Circulation of Insulin-Treated Subjects". J. Clin. Invest.; 35: 170–190.

The Nobel Prize in Physiology or Medicine 1977. Nobelprize.org. http:// nobelprize.org/nobel_prizes/medicine/laureates/1977/. Accessed June 22, 2011.

Some Review Articles on Medical Uses of RIA.

"Immunoassay of Protein Hormones," in *The Hormones: Physiology, Chemistry, and Applications*, v. 4, 557–630 (G. Pincus et al, eds. Academic Press, 1964).

"Heterogeneity of Peptide Hormones – Its Relevance in Clinical Radioimmunoassay," in *Advances in Clinical Chemistry*, v. 20, 1–47 (O. Bodansky and A. L. Latner, eds., Academic Press, 1978).

"Radioimmunoassay: Its Relevance to Clinical Medicine," in *Basic Research and Clinical Medicine* 3–22 (S. P. Bralow et al. eds., McGraw Hill, 1981).

"Radioimmunoassay in Oncology," *Cancer*, 53: 1426–1431 (1984).

Additional References

Straus, Eugene (1999). Rosalyn Yalow, Nobel Laureate: Her Life and Work in Medicine

Yalow, Rosalyn (1977). "Autobiography." Nobelprize.org

Stone, Elizabeth (1978), "A MME. Curie from the Bronx." Nytimes.com

Glossary

Accuracy: The closeness of mean test results to the true concentration of theanalyte.

Active Blocker: Such as HBR, which is a specific binder that is directed against the human heterophilic antibody.

Adsorption: the passive attachment of a liquid to a solid surface creating a thin film.

Affinity: Antibody affinity is typically represented by the equilibrium dissociation constant (Kd), a ratio of Koff/Konbetween the antibody and its antigen, where lower Kdvalue suggests higher affinity relationship.

Affinity Constant: Describes the binding interaction between antibody and antigen. Also known as association or equilibrium constant.

Affinity Purification: Column purification where specific antibody fraction binds to the antigen to which it is made.

Antibody: A Y-shaped protein on the surface of B cells that is secreted into the blood or lymph in response to an antigenic stimulus, such as a bacterium, virus, parasite, or transplanted organ, and that neutralizes the antigen by binding specifically to it; an immunoglobulin.

Antibody Light Chain Region: Either of the two smaller of the four polypeptide chains that are subunits of antibodies. They compose one half of the antigen binding sites of antibodies, together with the variable region of the heavy chain.

Antibody Heavy Chain Region: Either of the two larger of the four polypeptide chains comprising antibodies. They compose one half of the antigen binding sites of antibodies, together with the variable region of the light chain.

Antibody Variable/N Terminal Region: The binding site of antibodies located at the topmost tip of the "Y" arms of both Light and Heavy Chains. This variable region, composed of 110–130 amino acids, give the antibody its specificity for binding antigen.

Antibody Constant/C Terminal Region: The portion of the antibody shape that includes all except the topmost tips of the "Y" arms of both the Light and Heavy Chains. The constant region determines the mechanism used to destroy antigen. Antibodies are divided into five major classes, IgM, IgG, IgA, IgD and IgE, based on their constant region structure and immune function.

Antibody FAB Region: Top portion of antibody "Y" shape consisting of all the variable regions and a small portion of the constant region.

Antibody Fc Region: Bottom portion or stem of antibody "Y" shape consisting of the largest portion of the constant region.

Antigen: A substance that when introduced into the body stimulates the production of an antibody. Antigens include toxins, bacteria, foreign blood cells, and the cells of transplanted organs.

Antigen-Down Immunoassay: In an antigen-down immunoassay, the analyte is coated onto a 96-well microtiter plate (rather than an antibody) and used to bind antibodies found in a sample. When the sample is added (such as human serum), the antigen on the plate is bound by antibodies (IgE for example) from the sample, which are then retained in the well. A species-specific antibody (anti-human IgE for example) labelled with HRP is added next, which, binds to the antibody bound to the antigen on the plate. The higher the signal, the more antibodies there are in the sample.

Antigen-down assays can be configured as rapid tests and are often used to diagnose allergy conditions – routinely a patient's blood is tested against different allergens to see if the person has antibodies to that allergen.

Antiserum: Human or animal serum containing antibodies that are specific for one or more antigens.

Antistreptolysin O (ASO) Positive Human Serum: Antistreptolysin O, commonly called ASO, is an antibody found in human blood produced upon an infection by Group A Streptococcus bacterium.

In an infected individual, the Group A Streptococci produced Streptolysin O acts as a protein antigen and causes the patient's immune system to mount a defensive response with Antistreptolysin O antibodies. A rise in ASO titer level begins about 1 week after infection and peaks 2–3 weeks later. In the absence of complications or re-infection, the ASO titer will usually fall to pre-infection levels within 6–12 months. Approximately 80–85% of the patients who demonstrate a Group A Streptococcal infection will also demonstrate an elevated ASO titer.

Group A Streptococcus has caused more widespread diseases than any other group of bacteria. Upon initial infection by Group A Streptococcus, a patient may present with a sore throat and general malaise. However, there also exists a correlation between the initial illness and development of post-streptococcal syndromes. Of these, acute rheumatic fever and acute glomerulonephritis are the most debilitating. To determine if a streptococcal infection was the root cause, an Antistreptolysin O test is performed.

ASO titer determination can help distinguish beta-hemolytic Group A Streptococcal rheumatic fever from acute rheumatic diseases. A normal ASO reference range for adults is <100 Todd units or a 1: 99 dilution. The majority of physicians will order a differential diagnosis panel to be run on a sample consisting of ASO titer, C-Reactive Protein (CRP) and Rheumatoid Factor (Rf). Eighty percent of Group A Streptococcal infected patients also have elevated CRP levels greater than 1.2 mg/dL.

False positive ASO titers can be caused by increased levels of serum beta-lipoprotein produced in liver disease and by contamination of the serum with Bacillus cereus and Pseudomonas sp. ASO titers are elevated in 85% of patients with rheumatic fever but may not be elevated in cases involving skin or renal sequelae. A marked rise in titer or a persistently elevated titer indicates that a Streptococcus infection or post-streptococcal sequelae are present. Both clinical and laboratory findings should be correlated in reaching a diagnosis.

AP: (Alkaline Phosphatase): – phosphatase enzyme that removes a phosphate group from a substrate. In ELISAs the substrate is p-Nitro Phenyl Phosphate (pNPP).

Ascites: The accumulation of serous (of, relating to, producing, or resembling serum; especially having a thin watery constitution) fluid in the peritoneal cavity. Unpurified monoclonal antibody containing fluid drawn directly from hybridomas, grown within a living host (usually mice).

Assay diluent: (see also buffer): – buffer solution in which the sample to be analysed is diluted in.

Assay precision: – intra-assay and inter-assay coefficient of variability (CV)

Repeatability between samples ran on multiple assay plates (inter-assay CV) or the measure of each sample in duplicate for each analyte (intra-assay CV).

The inter-assay CV is an expression of plate-to-plate consistency that is calculated from the mean values for the high and low controls on each plate.

The intra-assay CV reported in these studies is an average value calculated from the individual CVs for all of the duplicates, even if the total number of samples requires the use of multiple assay plates.

Inter-assay % CVs of less than 15 are generally acceptable.

Intra-assay % CVs should be less than 10.

Assay sensitivity: – a measure of the ability of the ELISA to distinguish between small changes in concentration.

Autoantibody: – An antibody that reacts with the cells, tissues, or native proteins of the individual in which it is produced.

Background: – the signal readout attributable to all reagents excluding the analyte. Should be low.

Blocking: – application of reagents, generally buffers, to lower background by binding to the potential non-specific binding sites of antibodies and enzyme conjugates.

Buffer: – solutions containing compounds, generally proteins, to reduce the non-specific binding of antibodies; used in blocking to reduce background.

Cell Culture: The maintenance or growth of dispersed cells in a medium after removal from the body.

Cell Line: Cells grown in tissue culture and representing generations of a primary culture.

Coating/Capture antibody: – An anchored primary antibody used in ELISA procedures to bind an antigen in solution.

Competitive Inhibition immunoassay: Competitive inhibition assays are often used to measure small analytes because competitive inhibition assays only require the binding of 1 antibody rather than 2 as is used in standard ELISA formats. Because of the high probability for steric hindrance occurring when 2 antibodies attempt to bind to a small molecule at the same time, a sandwich assay format may not be feasible; therefore, a competitive inhibition assay would be preferable. In a sequential competitive inhibition assay, the sample and conjugated analyte are added in steps like a sandwich assay, while in a classic competitive inhibition assay, these reagents are incubated together at the same time.

In a sequential competitive inhibition assay format, a monoclonal antibody is coated onto a 96-well microtiter plate. When the sample is added, the MoAb captures free analyte out of the sample. In the next step, a known amount of analyte labelled with either biotin or HRP is added. The labelled analyte will then also attempt to bind to the MoAb adsorbed onto the plate; however, the labelled analyte is inhibited from binding to the MoAb by the presence of previously bound analyte from the sample. This means that the labeled analyte will not be bound by the monoclonal on the plate if the monoclonal has already bound unlabelled analyte from the sample. The amount of unlabelled analyte in the sample is inversely proportional to the signal generated by the labeled analyte. The lower the signal, the more unlabelled analyte there is in the sample. A standard curve can be constructed using serial dilutions of an unlabelled analyte standard. Subsequent sample values can then be read off the standard curve as is done in the sandwich ELISA formats.

The classic competitive inhibition assay format requires the simultaneous addition of labeled (conjugated analyte) and unlabelled analyte (from the sample). Both labeled and unlabelled analyte then compete simultaneously for the binding site on the monoclonal capture antibody on the plate. Like the sequential competitive inhibition format, the coloured signal is inversely proportional to the concentration of unlabelled target analyte in the sample. Detection of labeled analyte may be made by using a peroxidase substrate such as TMB, which can be read on a microtiter plate reader.

Conjugation: Attachment of a peptide segment to a carrier protein.

Cross-reactivity: – an antibody binding to a target that is very similar to but not the intended target analyte, i.e., a closely related molecule with structural similarities to the target antigen.

Defibrinated Plasma: Chemical treatment (defibrination) of plasma to cause clotting (needed due to the presence of anticoagulants that were added during blood collection). Then dialysis is performed to bring the biochemical values back into the normal range and remove sodium azide, residues, etc. This is a less expensive form of serum.

Detection limit: – the smallest quantity of analyte that can be reliably measured by the ELISA assay; it is often set to 2 standard deviations (2 SD) above background level.

Dilution: – addition of a buffer to a protein solution to make it less concentrated, used in optimizing antibody concentration but also applied to samples to obtain readings within the dynamic range of the assay.

Dynamic range: – range in the ELISA over which the absorbance reading increases in a linear mode and the analyte can be reliably measured.

Edge effect: – the result of inconsistencies in the production of ELISA multiwell plates or when assay conditions, such as stacking plates, cause the outer wells to behave differently. As a result, unexpected values can appear in the outer wells which may be out of line with neighbouring well. This can best be controlled for by using duplicates or triplicates for all samples, and noting any large variations in the results for a given sample.

Epitope: The surface portion of an antigen capable of eliciting an immune response and of combining with the antibody produced to counter that response.

Glomerulonephritis: A form of nephritis characterized by inflammation of the renal glomeruli.

Group A Streptococcus: A common but virulent streptococcus that damages the tissue it infects and produces toxins that trigger a form of shock that affects the vital organs.

HAMA: Human Anti Mouse Antibodies, a common form of heterophilic antibody that binds to mouse antibodies. Other heterophilic antibodies produced by humans that bind to other animal antibodies are similarly named, such as HAGA (Human Anti Goat Antibodies), HARA (Human Anti Rabbit Antibodies), etc.

Heterophilic Antibodies: Endogenous antibodies found in patients' serum/plasma which can bind to immunoglobulins of other species, including the species used to generate the antibodies used as reagents for immunoassays. These antibodies can interfere in immunoassays, causing a spurious elevation of measured value that is independent of the true analyte concentration, thus potentially misclassifying samples.

Heterophilic Blocking Reagent (HBR): A novel reagent which has been specifically designed to combat the problems of heterophilic interference in immunoassays.

Heterophilic interference: – arises from antibodies found in the sample analysed by the ELISA; it is binding by these antibodies to the detection antibody used in the assay. The best-known example of heterophilic interference is HAMA (human anti-mouse antibody) found in some patients where it interferes with the accurate analyte determination, showing false positive readings.

HRP (Horseradish Peroxidase): – an enzyme that breaks down hydrogen peroxide to water – a peroxidase. Chromogenic substrates such as TMB serve as indicators of that enzyme activity.

Hook effect: – caused by very high levels of antigen in the sample. As a result, specific binding of the antigen by the antibody is insufficient to match analyte levels and signal is lower than expected. The best way to avoid this issue is to test several dilutions of each sample.

Hybridoma: A cell that is produced in the laboratory from the fusion of an antibody-producing lymphocyte and a non-antibody producing cancer cell, usually a myeloma or lymphoma. It proliferates and produces a continuous supply of a specific monoclonal antibody.

Immunoassay: A laboratory technique that makes use of the binding between an antigen and its homologous antibody in order to identify and quantify the specific antigen or antibody in a sample.

Immunoglobulin: Any of a group of large glycoproteins that are secreted by plasma cells and that function as antibodies in the immune response by binding with specific antigens. There are five classes of immunoglobulins: IgA, IgD, IgE, IgG, and IgM.

Interference: – effects on the immunoassay that interfere with the accurate measurement of the analyte (e.g., matrix effect, heterophilic interference).

Matrix effect: – the effect compounds in the sample have on the measurement of the analyte.

In Vitro: In an artificial environment outside the living organism.

In Vivo: Within a living organism.

Iodination: The substitution or addition of iodine atoms containing radioactive isotopes used as a medical tracer.

Labeling/Detection/Tracer antibody: A primary antibody used in ELISA procedures to allow secondary antibody labelling of antigen.

Lyophilize: To freeze-dry (blood plasma or other biological substances).

Monoclonal antibody: Ofor relating to a protein from a single clone of cells, all molecules of which are the same.

pNPP (para-Nitrophenylphosphate): colorimetric substrate for alkaline phosphatase, it precipitates as a yellow substance.

Off The Clot (OTC): Clotting is allowed to occur naturally (without assistance of chemicals). This is a more expensive form of serum.

Peptide: A smallamino acid sequence used for generating sequence-specific antibodies.

Plasma: The fluid part of the blood remaining after centrifugation (removes blood cells, etc.), collected from patient into tube/bag containing anti-coagulants (i.e., EDTA, citrate, heparin, etc.) to prevent clotting of the fibrin in the blood.

Passive Blocker: Conventional blockers that use nonspecific substances (mouse IgG, Mouse Serum, nonspecific monoclonal antibodies, aggregated IgG, etc.) to block the binding of human heterophilic antibodies.

Polyclonal antibody: Produced by or being cells derived from two or more cells of different ancestry or genetic constitution. Multiple B cell response to an antigen resulting in a mixture of antibodies typically recognizing a variety of epitopes on the antigen.

Pre-immune serum: Blood serum extracted prior to an animal's immunization with an antigenic substance; often used as a control.

Primary antibody: An antibody produced in a host animal from a human antigen, such as Rabbit Anti Human PTH.

Protein stabilizers: Reagents that promote maintenance of the native structure of proteins during adsorption to the assay surface.

Rapid Test immunoassay: In addition to microtiter plates, immunoassays are also configured as rapid tests, such as a home pregnancy test. Like microtiter plate assays, rapid tests use antibodies to react with antigens and can be developed as MoAb-PoAb sandwich formats, competitive inhibition formats, and antigen-down formats. With a rapid test, the antibody and antigen reagents are bound to porous membranes, which react with positive samples while channelling excess fluids to a non-reactive part of the membrane.

Rapid immunoassays commonly come in 2 configurations: A lateral flow test where the sample is simply placed in a well and the results are read immediately. The flow through system requires placing the sample in a well, washing the well, and then finally adding an analyte-colloidal gold conjugate. The result is read after a few minutes, and one sample is tested per strip or cassette.

Because rapid tests are faster than microtiter plate assays, require little sample processing, are often cheaper, and generate yes/no answers without using an instrument, they are often used in the field by non-laboratory people testing whole samples. However, rapid immunoassays are not as sensitive nor can they be used to accurately quantitate an analyte. (Self-monitoring of blood glucose levels by diabetics is considered quantitative rapid testing; however, immunoassay technology is not used for these tests.) All rapid immunoassay tests can be converted to a microtiter plate assay, but not all microtiter plate assays can be converted to a rapid test.

Rheumatic Fever: A severe infectious disease occurring chiefly in children, characterized by fever and painful inflammation of the joints, and frequently resulting in permanent damage to the valves of the heart.

Rheumatoid Factor (RF): An autoantibody of high molecular weight that reacts against immunoglobulins of the class IgG and is often present in rheumatoid arthritis.

Sandwich immunoassay: In a typical microtiter plate sandwich immunoassay, a monoclonal antibody is adsorbed onto a plastic microtiter plate. When the test sample is added to the plate, the antibody on the plate will bind the target antigen from the sample, and retain it in the plate. When a polyclonal antibody is added in the next step, it also binds to the target antigen (already bound to the monoclonal antibody on the plate), thereby forming an antigen 'sandwich' between the two different antibodies. This binding reaction can then be measured by radio-isotopes, as in a radio-immunoassay format (RIA), or by enzymes, as in an enzyme immunoassay format (EIA or ELISA) attached to the polyclonal antibody. The radio-isotope or enzyme generates a colour signal proportional to the amount of target antigen present in the original sample added to the plate. Depending on the immunoassay format, the degree of colour can be detected and measured with the naked eye (as with a home pregnancy test), a scintillation counter (for an RIA), or with a spectrophotometric plate reader (for an EIA).

Secondary antibody: An antibody produced in an animal from an animal antigen, such as Goat Anti Rabbit IgG. They are used to detect the presence of a primary antibody.

Serum: The fluid part of blood remaining after removal of the fibrin. SLI provides two forms.

Specificity: The likelihood that the particular antibody is binding to a precise antigen epitope.

Substrate: – compound such as pNPP and TMB that is used to measure the analyte in an immunoassay.

Supernatant: Monoclonal antibody-containing fluid collected from hybridoma cell cultures.

TMB: – a colorimetric substrate for horseradish peroxidase, turning blue upon completion of the enzymatic reaction.

Whole Blood: Straight blood collection from a patient.

Glossary of Terms

AE Act: Atomic Energy Act 1962

AEC: Atomic Energy Commission

AERB: Atomic Energy Regulatory Board

ARPANSA: The Australian Radiation Protection and Nuclear Safety Agency

ASN: Nuclear Safety authority of France

BARC: Bhaba Atomic Research Centre

BRIT: Board of Radiation and Isotope Technology

C&SED: Civil and Structural Engg. Division

CANDU: Canada Deuterium Uranium

CCS: Cabinet Committee on Security

CNSC: Canadian Nuclear Safety Commission

CSS: Commission on Safety Standards

CT: Computed tomography

CWMF: Central Waste Management Facility

DAE: Department of Atomic Energy

DGSNR: Directorate General of Nuclear Safety and Radiation Protection

DRS: Directorate of Radiation Safety

ESL: Environmental Survey Laboratory

FCF: Fuel cycle facilities

GBq: Gigabecquerel

GSR: General Safety Requirement

HPU: Health Physics Unit

IAEA: International Atomic Energy Agency

IAEA-CRP: IAEA Coordinated Research Programme

IAEA-TECDOC: IAEA technical documents

ICRP: International Commission on Radiological Protection

IGRED: Industrial Gamma Radiography Exposure Device

INES: International Nuclear Event Scale

IPSD: Industrial Plants Safety Division

IRRS: Integrated Regulatory Review Service

IRS: Incident Reporting System

ITSD: Information and Technical Services Division

KAPP: Kakrapara Atomic Power Project

KGS: Kaiga Generating Station

KWH: Kilowawtt hour

MAPS: Madras Atomic Power Station

NAPS: Narora Atomic Power Station

Report No. 9 of 2012-13
Activities of Atomic Energy Regulatory Board 91

NPCIL: Nuclear Power Corporation of India Ltd.

NPP: Nuclear Power Plants

NPSD: Nuclear Projects Safety Division

NRF: Nuclear and Radiation Facilities

NSC: Nuclear Safety Commission of Japan

NSRA: Nuclear Safety Regulatory Authority

OECD: Organisation for Economic Co-operation and Development

OPSD: Operating Plants safety Division

PHWRs: Pressurised Heavy Water Reactors

PNRA: Pakistan Nuclear Regulatory Authority

RAPP: Rajasthan Atomic Power Project

RAPS: Rajasthan Atomic Power Station

RI: Regulatory Inspection

RIA: Radioimmunoassay

RPM: Radiation Protection Manual

RPR 2004: Atomic Energy (Radiation Protection) Rules, 2004

RRC: Regional Regulatory Centres

RSD: Radiological Safety Division

RSO: Radiological Safety Officer

SAAD: Safety Analysis and Documentation Division

SARCAR: Safety Review Committee for Application of Radiation

SARCOP: Safety Review Committee for Operating Plants

SRC: Safety Review Committee

SRI: Safety Research Institute

TAPS: Tarapur Atomic Power Station

US: United States of America

USNRC: United States Nuclear Regulatory Commission

WMD: Waste Management Division

WMD: Weapon of Mass Destruction

Abbreviations

Ach: Acetylcholine

ACTH: Adrino Cortico Trophic Hormone

ADH: Anti di Uretic Hormone

ADP: Adenosine Di Phosphate

ANS: Autonomic Nervous System

ATP: Adenosine Tri Phosphate

C: Cervical, cervical vertebrae, (C4 cervical vertebrae 4)

Cm: Centi meter

CNS: Central Nervous System

CRH: Corticotropin Releasing Hormone

CSF: Cerebro Spinal Fluid

DIT: Di Iodo Tyrosine

DNA: Deoxyribo Nucleic Acid /d: Per day

ECF: Extra Cellular Fluid

ER: Endoplasmic Reticulum

FSH: Follicular stimulating hormone g: Gram

GHIH: Growth Hormone Inhibiting Hormone

GHRH: Growth Hormone Releasing Hormone

GI: Gastro Intestinal

GnRH: Gondotrophin Releasing Hormone

HCG: Human Chorionic Gonadotrophin hormone

Hcl: Hydrochloric acid

hGH: Human Growth Hormone

ICSH: Interstitial Cell Stimulating Hormone

IGF: Insulin like Growth Factors

IUD: Intra Uterine Device

L: Lumbar, lumbar vertebrae, (L3, lumbar vertebrae 3)

L: Liter

LES: Lower oesophageal sphincter

LH: Luteinizing Hormone

LPH: Lipo tropic Hormone

M: Meter

MIT: Mono Iodo Tyrosine

ml.: Millilitre

mm: Milli meter

P: Phosphate

PBI: Protein Bound Iodine

PH: Power of Hydrogen

PIH: Prolactin Inhibiting Hormone

PNS: Peripheral Nervous System

POMC: Pro-Opio Melano Cortin

PRH: Prolactin Releasing Hormone

PTH: Para Thyroid Hormone

RNA: Ribo Nucleic Acid

rRNA: Ribosomal Ribo Nucleic Acid

T: Thoracic, thoracic vertebrae, (T1 thoracic vertebrae 1)

T3: Tri-iodothyronine

T4: Thyroxin

TGB: Tyro globulin

TRH: Thyrotropin Releasing Hormone

TSH: Thyroid Stimulating Hormone

UV: Ultra Violet